RETIRING RETIREMENT

A NEW ROADMAP FOR LONGEVITY AND QUALITY LIVING

Elmer H. Burack and
Marvin D. Burack

Brace-Park Press
Northbrook, Illinois

This book is not intended as a substitute for advice,
diagnosis, or treatment by a physician or other health
care practioner. Readers who feel or suspect that they
may have specific medical problems should consult a
physician about any suggestions made in this book.
This book presents numerous vignettes for illustrative
purposes. Any similarity to persons living or dead or
actual companies or organizations is purely coincidental
unless otherwise indicated.

TABLE OF CONTENTS

RETIRING RETIREMENT   ix

PREFACE   xi

ACKNOWLEDGEMENTS   xi

INTRODUCTION   xvii

PART I: RETIREMENT: AN HONORABLE BURIAL
AND NEW OPPORTUNITIES AND CHALLENGES

Chapter I – 1:
The "Invention" of Retirement and Ageism   1
    Overview   3
    The Retirement Ideology   4
    Retirement Thinking and Behavior 5
    Ageism in US Organizations   5

Chapter I – 2:
The New "You Bet Your Life" (with apologies to
Groucho Marx)   9
    The New "You Bet Your Life"
      (with apologies to Groucho Marx)   11
    Which Matters Most, Nature or Nurture?   13
    The Aging "Miracle"   14
    The "Miracle" and Quality of Living   16

Chapter I – 3:
Profiling the Aging Society   17
    Reframing Society: The New Second Adulthood   19
    Previewing Aging Myths and Realities   21
    Summary   22

PART II: SENSE MAKING: NEWER ROLES IN THE AGING SOCIETY (A NEW SECOND ADULTHOOD)

Chapter II –1:
Who's in Charge? Ready or Not, You Are in Charge! 25
    Where Did You Get Those Ideas? 27
    A Sense of Control 28

The Degree to Which People Feel in Control:
Where We Are Today 29
    A Health Revolution and New Health Care Roles 31
    - Creating a "New" Medicine 35
    Therapies for the Health Information Explosion 36
    - Research: Sorting Things Out 37
    - Types of Research 38

Chapter II – 2:
How Old Are You Really? Quality Age 43
    How Old Are You? Psychological Dimensions 45
    Uncommon Common Knowledge 47
    Aging, New Perspectives 49
    The New Second Adulthood 50

Chapter II – 3:
Characteristics of "Second Adulthood" People:
A Newer View of Age and Aging 53
    Background 55
    Looking at Age in Three Dimensions 57
    The Age Game 58
    Nature-Nurture Revisited: A Concluding Note 60

PART III: MAPPING HEALTH SUCCESS STRATEGIES

Chapter III – 1:
Background 65
 A Critical View of Individuals as Healthful
 Living Models 67

Chapter III – 2:
Mapping Health Success Strategies: Methods 71
 Mapping Health Success Strategies: Alternate
 Approaches 73
 Benchmarking and First Things First 75
 "Scorecard" Methods and Processes 78
 Applying a Scorecard Approach 78

Chapter III – 3:
**Mapping Health Success Strategies: Numerical
Approaches, Part #1** 83
 Introduction and Background:
  The Multiple Faces of Age and Aging 85
  "Let's Have a Picnic": An Application Example 86

Chapter III – 4:
**Mapping Health Success Strategies:
Numerical and Other Approaches, Part #2** 91
 Introduction 93
 Physical and Biological Age: A Note 98

PART IV: PASSAGES: YOUR PASSPORT TO THE FUTURE

Chapter IV – 1:
Trip Planning   102
   Introduction   103
   Mind-Body Health Myths:
      The Old Aging Paradigm   104
   The New Aging Paradigm   106
   Trip Planning in Perspective   110

Chapter IV – 2:
A Framework for Personal Change   111
   A Game Plan for Personal Change   113
   The Change Framework: "AIMS"   114
   The "AIMS" for Change Framework:
      A Concluding Note   119

Chapter V – 1:
Introduction to the "5R's"
Lifestyle and Financial Security Planning   121

Chapter V – 2:
The Financials, Health Care and Women's Issues   137
   Selected Bibliography: The Financials   155

Chapter V – 3:
Spirituality   157

Chapter V – 4:
A New "Path – Second Adulthood"   177

Chapter V – 5:
Planning for a Second Adulthood   187

Chapter V – 6:
Sorting Things Out and Making Decisions   201

Chapter V – 7:
School Was Never Like This:
The New World of Lifelong Learning   211

Chapter V – 8:
The Personal Computer and World Wide Web:
Your Link to the Future   223

POSTSCRIPT   231

BIBLIOGRAPHY   233

REFERENCE NOTES   243

Preface

Why a book on "retirement" when we seem to be living in a new era of robustness, individual vitality and dynamic change? The robustness and dynamic change are really at the heart of the issue and one key reason for this book. There is so much change going on that no clear idea has emerged for "life after retirement" nor even the more basic questions as to distinctions between "old" and "older", nor whether "retirement" is even a relevant term or concept any more. In the traditional society we are rapidly leaving behind, "retirement" was a major life-marker; for those who survived! In no uncertain terms it announced the withdrawal from full-time work. Modest ceremonies and celebrations marked the occasion. "Free at last"; to golf, fish, work part-time, vegetate, read or travel. It proclaimed to family, friends, government offices and insurance firms that you were now officially in a new role, most often around 65 years of age. Financial benefits "kicked in". People "now" had to fend for themselves. Businesses, school systems and employers generally were absolved of responsibilities for your future. Years ago, if ever, our society withdrew any special mark of respect or acknowledgment of wisdom for those who retired. Each person had to figure it out for himself/herself. People seemed to be on a downward slide reflected in aging characteristics. Appearance, abilities, memory and nasty diseases all seemed to "pile up" and were part of the picture. In the newly emerging society we can do much better...we *are* doing much better than this!

A second reason for writing this book is the mixed message all of us are receiving. Everyone has an older family member or friend who is *experiencing* perhaps the worst of times in his/her life; Alzheimer's, serious heart and circulatory problems, a terrible disease or the aftermath of long-term body abuse from smoking and/or drinking. Yet on television and daily in our favorite newspapers and magazines, we hear about those sensational people, leading robust lives at 70,80 or 90 years of age and the fast growing legion of those over 100. Are the latter isolated incidents or a growing trend in the "new" society? If the stories are credible, how does the individual take advantage of these possibilities especially since everybody knows that there's no such thing as a "free ride"?

A third point in undertaking this writing is the fact that tens of thousands and perhaps millions can already certify the death of "retirement" and are already experiencing a new and unique life role, although the dimensions of this new lifestyle are ill defined. Thus, identifying newer individual possibilities and next steps, expanding individual awareness and exploding deeply ingrained myths about aging provide a powerful additional rationale for this undertaking.

A final point is the fact that some 10,000 "Baby Boomers" are pouring over the middle age "start line" daily. Many have only thought superficially about "thriving after 55" in a world where they are likely to live into their late 80's and with reasonably good health. In the aging game, the Baby Boomers have the greatest degrees of freedom and choice in health and financial matters relative to other age cohorts who have already moved on into their 60's, 70's and 80's. These writings will help these readers think through and critically examine realistic lifestyle and career options.

We are grateful to dozens of social scientists, researchers and members of the health care community and writers whose published ideas and findings are referenced throughout this material. Also, many have provided thoughtful comments and feedback. They are noted on the following pages. We also wish to acknowledge the hundreds of men and women who shared their stories in countless encounters and in personal and continuing education formats.

Acknowledgements

As authors, we gratefully acknowledge the contributions of numerous individuals and organizations in developing this book. Many gave generously of their time and shared both experiences and ideas. Also, some of those with whom we had been in contact left a remarkable trail of writings which were critical in developing these ideas and these are appropriately referenced. "New age" perspectives and the mind-body spirit connection capture both the depth and breadth of the underlying assumptions and discussions in our book *Retiring Retirement*.

Almost a decade has passed since we started to sort through and attempted to digest literally hundreds of writings and personal experiences in order to piece together newer directions of "retirement" developments. Aside from research reports, books and many other writings, we have identified a representative group of practitioners, researchers, executives and specialists whose work (further) fleshed out the ideas and approaches described here. We apologize in advance for neglecting to list many others due to time and space limitations.

For our purposes, the following individuals played major roles in shaping the discussions. These include, with some key publication dates: Herbert Benson ("Relaxation response and application's," 1975; Bernie Siegel ("self-healing," 1986); Ken Dychtwald ("Age Wave and boomers", 1989, 1999); Anthony Robbins ("Unlimited Power," 1992); Deepak Chopra ("Ageless Body, Timeless Minds," 1993), and who with David Sina does it again in "Growing Younger and Living Longer (2001); Zalman Schachter-Shalomi ("Age-ing to Sage-ing™," 1995); Mathew Fox ("Reinventing Work and spirituality applications" 1994 and 2000); Andrew Weil ("Natural Health and living healthfully," (1995, 2000); Gail Sheehy ("New Passages," 1995); Daniel Goleman ("Emotional Intelligence and applications" 1995, 1999); Richard Restak ("The Brain," 1995); James S. Gordon ("Medicine's New Manifesto," 1996); and Michael Roizen (Real Age," 1999).

Other writers, social scientists and professionals instrumental in establishing a foundation for our discussions included William Graebner ("Retirement Trends," 1980), and Elizabeth Lesser ("The New Spirituality," 1999). Alan Pifer and Lydia Bronte, editors, collected a highly useful group of papers which helped to define critical aspects of the aging society (1986).

We must also acknowledge the forward thinking of Horace Deets, former Executive Director of AARP. He provided general support to a remarkable, multi-year series of University Teaching/Research Colloquia (1994-1998) focused on senior employment and aging issues. It was also during his "watch" that we came to fully appreciate the enormous impact of some 75 million "Baby Boomers" on retirement matters. Many are already members of AARP. A special note of thanks is also due Joan Kelley, a Senior Employment Administrator with AARP before her retirement, who helped to organize and administer the "University Teaching/Research Colloquia" (Washington, D.C.). These helped to highlight employment, work and performance matters. She was also instrumental for research purposes, in helping to open many corporate doors and gaining access to key foundations and institutions fostering aging, performance and employment studies.

We would also like to identify a representative group of institutions and individuals who provided forums for both shaping and refining our aging thinking. Some also resulted in hands-on opportunities for us to "performance test" newer ideas and processes. These included: the Spiritual Eldering Institute; the Lifelong Learning Society with notable programs at Florida Atlantic University and Northwestern University including its Institute For Learning in Retirement; the Oasis and North Shore Learning Centers (Northbrook, IL and Northfield, IL) respectively; the Cancer Wellness Center (Northbrook, IL); Elder Hostel; the "Unlimited Power" seminars (Anthony Robbins); Moshe Feldenkrais; and Jose Silva.

Before closing these acknowledgement notes, we would like to recognize the efforts of a small group of Organization Behavior Teaching Society (OBTS) members who maintained a long standing interest in aging matters. Through their loose network, they helped to develop an OBTS conference agenda which led to informative discussions and useful personal information over a period of many years. The group included: Gil Boyer, Andre Delbecq, Dick Daft, Steve Fink, Fran Hall, Harvey Kolodny, Nick Mathys, Steve Robbins, Jeff Sonnenfeld, Judi Strauss, and Joan Weiner. One of the authors, Elmer Burack, also had the good fortune to be a part of this group for many years.

Though we have had the benefit of this large group of insightful individuals and institutions, we as authors must assume responsibility for the final product. This we do.

Elmer Burack, Marvin Burack
January 2002
Chicago, IL.

Introduction

The "aging society" is already here with effects becoming more evident daily. Almost 10,000 Baby-Boomers per day, on the average, are crossing the 55 years of age marker. Clearly, they have a major stake in these developments. Also, the population segment of those over 85 years of age is the fastest growing and those reaching the 100-year marker will shortly hit 100,000. Millions are already reshaping the "retirement" experience. For those (still) employed, many employers for the first time are starting to seriously study both the opportunities and the problems of a workplace that is aging and non-retiring or in a semi-retirement mode. These have enormous implications for employment relationships, benefits and shaping a whole new employment relationship.

Since this is a dynamic area of change affecting most all, each person will have to assume a new level of responsibility in critically examining these developments and fashioning his/her own life plan.

Those already in a "semi-retirement" or "retirement" mode are finding that the terms and understandings of "retirement," learned in early years, no longer apply. "Retirement" is literally being retired and many new modes of planning and living life are emerging for Boomers and older population segments. This writing summarizes some of the most important changes taking place which are affecting more mature population members (say 55+). It provides a comprehensive schema for viewing these changes from an individual perspective and presents a number of approaches to help in putting together an action agenda customized to individual needs.

Almost daily, the "evidence" mounts that individuals have a remarkable opportunity to shape the quality of their lives, and arguably, their longevity as well. Even the old adage "it's never too late to learn (and to do!)" turns out to be a valid point. Almost one-third of senior citizens now have some familiarity with the computer and are turning out in fast growing numbers for a myriad of life-long learning activities. Indeed, it is never too late to learn and to do! On the other hand, there are some long-held assumptions and beliefs that are slowing many in taking advantage of these new possibilities. These need to be critically examined. A favorite one relates to inherited traits, "genes".

"It's in the genes" or "It runs in the family". Either one says pretty much the same thing. Most all of us have probably said this at one time or another. In reality, all of us are players in a high stakes game of life. According to the rules of the traditional "game", it was showdown, open face, five-card, no draw poker. "We played the hand we got dealt". Heart attacks, overweight, longevity and good health or poor health were largely predetermined for us in the "game" of life. So, why fight it? These beliefs were especially prominent among the "GI Generation" (those born approximately between 1915-1927) which preceded the Baby-Boomers (born approximately between 1946 and 1965). Insurance actuaries and the medical profession often seemed to provide plenty of support for these attitudes. They became entrenched.

Few except some social scientists and statisticians seemed to notice some remarkable societal changes taking place that would change game rules. These would lead to descriptive terms such as "the aging society" and the "new age" signaled by the millennium. A new "game of life" was in the making.

Note:

This book is intended as reference material. It is not to be considered a medical manual. The approaches given here are designed to help people make informed decisions about their health and quality of life. It is not intended as a substitute for any treatment that may have been prescribed by your physician or health practioner.

Part I provides the following discussions and resource ideas:

- The "Invention" of Retirement and Ageism
- The New You Bet Your Life (with apologies to Groucho Marx)
- The Aging Miracle
- A Profile of the Aging Society

PART I

Retirement–
An Honorable Burial and New
Opportunities and Challenges

Chapter I - 1

The "Invention" of Retirement
and Ageism

OVERVIEW

It required almost 100 years to assemble the myriad of pieces comprising "retirement". It solidified in the post World War II era. No wonder, its parts and contributors were drawn from all areas of society: political, philosophical, economic, social, technological and ideological. It was assembled with philosophical underpinnings that "benefited" from statesmen, corporate leaders, scholars, engineers and union bosses. Insurance companies were quick to note the income opportunities of pension funds. Federal legislation and special IRS regulations and allowances assured "retirement's" durability and widespread applicability. Its coming of age and institutionalization was further signaled by scholarly historical works such as William Graebner's *History of Retirement in the Unites States* (1980)[1]. The formal "corporate seal of approval" by General Motors' President Charles Wilson in 1950 and the "green light" for the union's collective bargaining activity and negotiation brought powerful retirement allies together. By the 1960's, everything seemed to be in place. In a world of slow change that would probably have been a relatively happy end to a rather long story. Trouble was that "retirement," as it finally evolved in the United States at that time, was *already obsolete*. The *Aging Society*[2] of the 1990's, 2000 and beyond was already a statistical fact. Fast emerging advances in health care delivery and technology and massive life style changes led to dramatic increases in length of life expectations and improvements in the quality of living. At the same time these posed new issues in employment, productivity and quality of life. Gail Sheehy's Passages for the 1970's and 1980's was out of date so that the *New Passages* (1994)[3] became a logical and needed reconstruction of the life at work-end phenomenon. Work-end, "recareering", "renewal", "protirement" and "Age-ing to Sage-ing™"[4] were part of a whole new vocabulary that social scientists, scholars and theologians were trying to fit to these rapidly changing circumstances.

THE RETIREMENT IDEOLOGY

A newer ideology of retirement was legitimized and institutionalized in the years subsequent to World War II. Technological change spurted. Retirement became liberal capitalism's answer to technological job displacement and seemingly a solution to a threatened long term labor surplus.[5] It facilitated disengagement from the workplace and getting plugged into a fast growing network of institutions and programs dedicated to serving retired people. Corporations, labor unions and insurance companies were major parties in legitimizing the concept and processes, establishing retirement benefit structures including pensions, and "lobbying-in" anti-age discrimination legislation. The traditional advantages of pension systems that promoted efficiency, employment stability and job security were interlaced throughout the fast growing collectively bargained plans and retirement structures. Private plan coverage of almost 10 million workers in 1950 was more than double that in 1940.[6] In subsequent years, over 40 percent of workers were covered. Embedded within these developments was a subtle and continuing affirmation that *older people, especially those over sixty-five, were incapable or/and unwilling to work!* Also included was the notion that mandatory retirement was a needed and important strategic business prerogative, especially of large business corporations. The general lack of gerontological research and reliable job analysis and performance knowledge, further encouraged the retention of untested aging assumptions and growth of aging myths.[7] The retirement mindset "hardened".

RETIREMENT THINKING AND BEHAVIOR

Retirement at 65 seemed logical...if one survived! It became a "natural" time for workforce disengagement, enjoying one's (few) remaining years, and winding up one's affairs. There was little reason to question the underlying assumptions and beliefs and thus to act otherwise. The medical profession emphasized disease prevention (e.g. measles, small pox) and health restoration. Insurance agents emphasized life (or "death") insurance to protect one's loved ones; perfectly natural in a one bread-winner family. Instances of longevity were in the "believe it or not" category. In brief, people lived out their beliefs; one's genes accounted for long life and short life spans as well.

However, there was also a darker side to the institutionalization of retirement. In a fast growing youth oriented culture, fertile conditions for ageism grew.

AGEISM IN U.S. ORGANIZATIONS AND SOCIETY

Ageism, individual bias expressed purely because of an age criterion, has shown remarkable durability. Its persistence is even more remarkable because it flies in the face of a fast growing body of contrary scientific evidence, ignores massive changes in institutional processes and structures, and even defies the common sense test of sight and experience. On the other hand, perhaps it is not so astonishing when past events, circumstances and time factors are examined.

Decades were required to scatter the seeds of ageism throughout U.S. industry, political and public administration units, and educational and health care institutions. It was nurtured in the late 1800's and early years of the 1900's by Frederick Winslow Taylor's brand of "Scientific Management". This approach to organization and management linked the theoretical and empirical constructs of economists, engineers and physicians to the workplace.[8] In the years prior to World War II, age discrimination worsened because of continued technological changes in industry favoring physical endurance, the widespread youth culture of the 1920's, and depression unemployment. Ageism assumptions became locked into the national political fabric through the continuing pressure of the efficiency advocates, the Civil Service Retirement Act of 1920[9], the Railroad Retirement Act, the Social Security Act of 1935[10], and the institutionalization of the pension concept as an efficiency/employment strategy.[11] Ageism became so ingrained as to serve as a business and general ideology; its assumptions were "common knowledge" by the forties. This inventory of "common knowledge" contained aging correlates such as: lack of adaptability and reluctance to change; rigidity, impatience and conservatism; inability to learn new things; and those who were burned-out or afflicted with fragile or poor health.[12]

Age Discrimination in Employment legislation (1967) reinforced national "equal opportunity" commitments but failed to set forth newer age correlates which would refute extant policies and practices in place for almost 100 years. Ageism simply became less visible, but it colored the assumptions and attitudes of numerous leaders, owners, administrators and managers. It was even woven into our social fabric. It received continuing reinforcement within the family and various other social and religious institutions. The incredible population bulge of the "baby-boomers" (1946-1965) gave substance and power to the youth culture and youth-driven decisions of the 1970's and 1980's. Equally compelling and massive changes would have to take place in industry's make-up and society generally, before a realistic and relevant age ideology would emerge. Events in the closing decades of the century met the prescribed needs.

Chapter I - 2

The New "You Bet Your Life"
(with apologies to Groucho Marx)

What if you had been invited to participate in the new TV game "You Bet Your Life" (with apologies to Groucho Marx), in which everybody is a winner? You can't lose. You and your family or valued other half are flown to a conveniently proximate major city most any time of the year (your choice) for a wonderful all-expense paid weekend. Of course there are also the big payoff show prizes, often worth tens of thousands of dollars. Interested? "Yes", most would respond.

You check things out and learn that this is for real! So, what's the "catch"? Uh-huh. You learn that there are three different contests ("A", "B" and "C" categories) during each game. So what's the difference? It turns out that the "odds" of winning in each category are different:

"A" Category	"B" Category	"C" Category
3 out of 10 or 30% of the time you win and 70% of the time the "house" wins.	5 out of 10 or 50% of the time you win and 50% of the time the "house" wins.	7 out of 10 or 70% of the time you win and 30% of the time the "house" wins.

Well, you've been to Las Vegas (or Atlantic City or to one of those riverboats), so you know that the payoffs must be different for each "category". Where the odds favor you (the "C" Category), the payoff must be small. Where the odds are against you (the "A" Category), that will most likely be the big payoff. It is logical, it only stands to reason. It makes perfectly good gambling sense!

Right. So the choice comes down to payoffs, the odds of winning and lots of personal factors.

But, what if you were then told that this was a *very different* "You Bet Your Life" game? The big payoff is in the "C" Category where the odds favor you! 70 percent of the time you come up a winner and you get the big payoff besides! Wow! Unless you like self-inflicted pain and anguish, the obvious choice is "C".

Well, the big payoff we are discussing in this chapter is quality of living (QL) and potentially, longevity as well. By QL, we mean feeling reasonably well, being able to move and function to the extent your body permits. It also means being able to go up "that" flight of stairs without huffing and puffing and to enjoy the best health possible whatever your circumstances. *The message of this chapter is that "today" you are in a much better position to determine many QL outcomes for yourself.* "Nurture" now plays a more important role than "Nature". In a comparatively short period of time, perhaps 50 years, the odds have shifted perceptions from being able to affect your QL outcomes in maybe 30 percent of individual circumstances to perhaps 70 percent, *if you are willing to take advantage of numerous advances in health self-management and mind-body technology.* In other words, most people can now influence many more of their QL outcomes and potentially, longevity as well. Does this mean everybody? No. Genes and one's nature still play an important role in these outcomes, though not as large as once thought.

The payoff is highly attractive but achieving the payoff does not come easily. Often lifestyle changes are called for and many have not gotten the message or sought out the message until confronted with some type of personal (often health-related) crisis or bad news regarding a close friend or family member. However, so many people today have been sensitized to these issues that individual adaptation is more easily undertaken.

It is now clear that the new "game of life" is big stakes with potentially important payoffs for all. It is important that all have a better understanding of the circumstances changing "game" structure and payoffs. Changing one's diet, habits or attitudes are challenging. But, the number of those who have already successfully made the transition, is growing rapidly. The realities of personal change are addressed in a subsequent chapter.

WHICH MATTERS MOST, NATURE OR NURTURE?

For many years, biologists and social scientists hotly debated the question as to whether biology or environment played a greater role in determining behavior.[1] Nearly lost from view but of great concern for all of our lives is the connection between the debate issues and advances in the medical and biological science communities that have greatly affected QL and longevity. For example, it has been well established that long life and good health are affected by our genes. But statisticians and others who study these things tell us that in the last 20 to 30 years, longevity has dramatically improved and that the odds favoring a life span of 80, 90 or even 100 are improving rapidly. What's going on? Are our genes changing all that fast? Hardly! So, we really have to critically examine "nurture", albeit, beyond traditional ideas. Also, we must view the role individual behavior plays in this picture. For our purposes, "nurture" reflects underlying social and economic conditions and massive changes in medical and mind-body technology. The latter includes remarkable advances in assimilating the wisdom of the ages and integrating these with a fast growing body of experience. This has been increasingly documented by a "new age conscious" medical doctors and social scientists. The "behaviors" being focused on are the *choices people make* in critical areas such as life-style, relationships, communications, nutrition and exercise. Especially of concern are the factors that clearly affect our health, quality of living (QL) and, arguably, longevity as well.

As an aside, intelligence ("IQ") figured prominently in traditional nature-nurture debates. Although social scientists pretty well established the contribution of genes (nature or heredity) to above-average intelligence (IQ), we have learned that *emotional intelligence* is the critical factor in a successful life, not IQ.[2] We are more interested in those aspects of intelligence which affect quality of life (and longevity) behaviors. Daniel Goleman's contributions to our understandings of "emotional intelligence" fit our needs admirably. The practical sides of intelligence for our purposes are the experiences and wisdom-driven behaviors that build our health, vitality and zest for living. Also, relationships play a key role here. Much more on this is discussed in a later section.

THE AGING "MIRACLE"

It took decades to unfold. It is still going on. Nobody is sure exactly when it started nor when it will end. What we are sure of is that its effects are likely to be felt universally and that it will impact virtually every phase of our lives. Historians, demographers and social scientists will be trying to sort it all out for years to come. It is no wonder that millions are still ignorant of its existence and fail to reap its potential benefits even though both the quality of life and "length of our days" are affected. At first blush it seems almost impossible to believe that such obvious benefits are accessible to many, perhaps most. Viewed more critically, perhaps it isn't all that mysterious. After all, the four-minute mile in the record book stood for years; it "couldn't be broken"! Then, in 1956, Roger Bannister did it! What is much less well known but of even wider significance is that over 30 other milers broke the four-minute time in the following years. With good reason the historian views events retrospectively, typically independent of current events or changes. Not so with the "aging miracle"; it is a part of all of our lives and still going on. Relatively few have known how to interpret events they have read about or witnessed or even experienced! For example, our wives' tennis groups include several octogenarians. W. Edward Deming, one of the fathers of the Total Quality movement, carried out an active lecture and travel schedule through his 80's and even into the 90's. Both Presidents Bush and Reagan were well into their 70's as leaders of our country. President Carter is said to be making some of the greatest contributions in his life though well into his 70's. He stays active physically, mentally and emotionally. Since individual circumstances and anecdotal experiences vary so widely, these *Chronicles* have provided demographic patterns to gain a sense of the big picture, and the general direction and thrust of massive societal change currently under way.

THE "MIRACLE" AND QUALITY OF LIVING

Embedded within the quality and length of life are a variety of experiences for which most individuals are able to exercise a surprising degree of influence. For a moment set aside the lengthening of life span as discussed earlier and let's focus on *quality of life*. Consider two key dimensions, one psychological, the other a combination of biological and physiological.[3] The former would include a positive outlook on things, a sense of contributing or making a difference, and a growing sense of fulfillment as opportunities to exercise wisdom or insights into life increase. In brief, a sense of happiness or contentment is a solid indication of a fulfilling quality of life. The latter would include various of the following possibilities: physical strength, endurance, eyesight and hearing acuity, ability to meet life's functional requirements (lifting, walking, sorting), memory, relative freedom from chronic disease or major illnesses and good "snap back" ability. In brief, everyday living without major limitations.

Reality and "Options"

After sifting through a wealth of anecdotal and research information, the following appears to be solid information as of this writing:

1) Age has become a poor predictor for the timing of life events, health, and family status among others. Interests, needs and values and possibilities, cannot be inferred from age alone.

2) Healthfulness is seen as increasingly central to quality of life, and considered to be a variable rather than"fixed" aspect of living.

3. Vast numbers of all Baby Boomers, men and women, express little interest in retirement as such.

4. Obesity and lack of sound nutrional knowledge threaten the quality of life of a virtually all aging components, but remarkable opportunities exist to deal with these.

5) Half of all people 75 to 84, report no major health limitations in everyday life activities.

6) Even for those over 84, more than one-third report no major health limitation in everyday life activities, although this may have occurred at some time in the past.[4]

Chapter I – 3

Profiling the Aging Society

RETIRING RETIREMENT

An age wave of unprecedented scope is rapidly taking shape that promises enormous societal changes, especially in the roles and attributions of older, old, and aging. A *"second adulthood society"* is an electrifying but realistic assessment of the nature of huge changes already underway. Ages 55 through 65 will merely represent a transitional passage to this society of new possibilities for older adults in our society. This chapter provides a preview of some highlights of the new demographics, and key myths and realities of aging. Much more detail is provided in subsequent chapters.

REFRAMING SOCIETY: THE SECOND ADULTHOOD

Career and life planning are being rapidly redefined in a society that is realistically described as a *"second adulthood society"*. The fastest growing age group consist of those 85 years of age and older. They already number some 3 million Americans and are expected to increase to 12 million by 2040. Even those 100 years of age and older have reached great numbers and will reach 100,000 in a few short years. The entire upper end of the age spectrum is growing as witnessed by those 65 years of age and older.

In just two decades, approximately one out of five people will be 65 years of age or older. For the large numbers of "Baby Boomers" who will be rapidly swelling these ranks, possibilities will be rapidly transformed into realities. A critical mass of men and women has already been attained. Sufficient numbers of mature people with common purposes now exist to facilitate, even encourage, rapid individual transformation and reaching out for a market basket of individual activities and possibilities. The following summary statistics for the 65 years of age and older population (in millions) suggest how rapidly the new age wave is moving through society. These figures indicate that one out of five people are likely to be in the folds of the second adulthood:

1900	1990	2000	2010	2020	2035
3	33	38	41	55	70

Reframing one's life will encompass every important aspect of life from food and clothing to travel and health, to continuing education and re-education, work, creative "personal" uses of the computer and social relationships and family. For those deeply involved with children or caretaker responsibilities in the past, mostly women, the degree of change possibilities will be great.

According to Linda Edelstein (1999)[1], the challenge of women's experience at mid-life will be increasingly developmental in nature. Women will possess the potential to move through three (healthy!) developmental phases. In the first, women relinquish older roles and activities and generally divorce themselves of older ways which have become burdensome and non-productive. This liberating action frees them up to enjoy the present moment, further introspection and thus get reconnected with themselves and their possibilities. This reconnection is the flavor of phase two. As phase two progresses, individuals will be able to focus on the future (phase three), a future involving newer roles, relationships, activities and work. Phases two and three are likely to also characterize some of the primary tasks of older adult males if they are to gain some of the real possibilities of the new second adulthood; it will not happen automatically. A conscious, determined effort will be required if these transformations are to be successful.

characteristic of the second adulthood will be new area living patterns. It has already become clear that some 50 percent of the older population 65 years of age and older is concentrated in nine states. California has over 3 million and Florida and New York each have 2 million. Six other states, Illinois, Michigan, New Jersey, Ohio, Pennsylvania and Texas, each have over 1 million.

PREVIEWING AGING MYTHS AND REALITIES

The viewpoint taken in this book is that both quality and length of life are twin objectives for the new second adulthood. Thus, it is of interest to reaffirm current truths, strip out and discard aging myths and build on these as a solid platform for future thinking and planning. This section chronicles selected themes; important ones are taken up in much greater detail in subsequent chapters.

1) Gender and Survival. Women tend to outlive men by an average of 8 years. Thus, for the 65 years of age and older group, there are three women for each two men! It is also well to recognize that the health of many women of advanced age leaves much to be desired. Thus, quality and length of life considerations will call for important developmental and health related actions by women.

2) Health Care. Since older people use a disproportionately large part of health care services and with the large scale reorganization of health care delivery, quality length of life criteria will call for the individual to increasingly take charge of managing their health care needs. People

will need to understand eating matters and nutrition, the role of exercise and the fit and exploitation of "alternative health care" processes. Individuals will be in partnership with their doctors, and, as in most partnerships, will be a "contributing" person in this relationship.

3) Incidence of Disease. Arthritis is a fact of life for perhaps one out of two of the over 65 population. It could be a problem for perhaps one out of four. Although cancer is given much press, heart disease and circulatory problems are far more widespread.

Although the aged are frequently characterized as being unhealthy or incapable of carrying out normal activities, some four out of five are healthy enough to engage in normal activities. With the growing number of second adulthood people, certain afflictions such as Alzheimer's will gain further prominence. Currently 20 to 25 percent of those over 80 develop Alzheimer's disease; the high priority assigned to medical research in this area seems likely to have a notable (positive) impact on this disease in the future.

SUMMARY

The aging society is already upon us. It gives promise of some remarkable possibilities for combining length of life and quality of life goal accomplishments. Baby Boomers who are the catalysts for these current and unprecedented changes are being challenged to assume new and deterministic roles in bringing about a new "second adulthood" characterized by good health *and* long life.

PART II

Sense Making:
Newer Aging Society Roles

Chapter II - 1

Who's in Charge?
Ready or Not, You Are in Charge!

WHERE DID YOU GET THOSE IDEAS?

There is no question that much of our view of life today was shaped by our past experience. For many, perhaps most, "past experience" included family, friends and the circumstances under which we were "brung up". Getting beat up, seemingly for no good reason; an early death of a brother, sister or parent; wealth or lack of it; good health or a long string of childhood illnesses; and/or the guys we hung out with, were all primary experiences shaping our views of the world, its possibilities and limitations. Of course, primary life experiences also included going off to war or passionate war protests; long, happy marriages or a string of divorces; and moving which meant permanently pulling up stakes and starting over with friends, business associates and churches, among others. All of this was like laying the foundation for a new home. Parameters of location, size and even eventual strength of the subsequent structure and its ability to withstand severe weathering, were importantly established by the artistry, thoughtfulness and experience expressed in the "foundation".

To carry this construction analogy further and get to one of the key points, think about what it takes to construct a housing addition. It may simply mean tacking the addition onto the existing structure. This strategy is much less complex than, say, wanting to add an additional floor and then finding out that the "foundation" will not support it. That is, when there is a need to radically alter or change our circumstances, it is back to the "drawing board". Trouble is that in our experience and that of many social scientists, *we may not know when it's time to go back to the drawing board!* Often the bugles don't blow and the fire alarm doesn't ring. Many changes take place around us without our hardly even being aware of it! Yet the cumulative effect of these and the need to respond to altered circumstances or the new responsibilities that must be taken on, are completely missed. Transition into the new millennium has brought forth a wealth of studies summarizing the amazing changes of the past decades. These studies make it quite clear that change has indeed touched all of us and perhaps in ways which we only partially understand and which go much beyond common knowledge. Another point is that new information and practices are now accessible; these may greatly improve the quality of our life and length of our days. These are the messages of this chapter.

A SENSE OF CONTROL

A person's sense of control and being able to cope show up repeatedly as critical factors in successful aging.[1] These factors cut a wide path across the health and aging scene. For quality of life (QL) and longevity this would include the growing need and reality of a *person managing their own health care*. The days of the doctor as friend, appointment maker and medical dispenser are largely gone. Much more on this in a later section.

Control and coping as related to aging includes numerous areas, the sum total of which is hopefully *successful* aging. Independence in transportation, shopping, work performance and household maintenance, are typical ingredients of a daily repetitive cycle. In health specific areas, control may mean: slowing normal aging processes[2] or actually improving functional capabilities such as endurance or weightlifting ability. It may also mean heading off major diseases through regular check-ups or dealing with the possible loss of bodily functions and mental or intellectual functioning. Social relations, number and frequency of contacts represent a still additional area in which individual control is enacted. Thus an individual's sense of control and ability to cope draw on numerous diverse activities. Factually, we may be "doing better" on some activities than in others. The grand total of these feelings linked to diverse areas and activities adds up to our *sense of control*, though we may assign higher priority to some over others.

It is critically important, however, to recognize *who or what sets the limits of the possible!* We have plenty of studies of the negative side of aging, but too few of the positive consequences of increasingly well established interventions and coping approaches! This book aims to re-right this balance. We want to bring to the reader a more comprehensive picture of strategies affecting our sense of well-being, QL and even longevity, so that *retiring retirement* becomes an eagerly awaited opportunity.

THE DEGREE TO WHICH PEOPLE FEEL IN CONTROL: WHERE WE ARE "TODAY"

Research results from a large scale study sheds light on several of the critical questions raised in this section. The research on "Successful Midlife Development" was sponsored by the prestigious John D. and Catherine T. MacArthur Foundation. Almost 3500 respondents from a national probability sample were interviewed and about 3000 of these returned questionnaires. Of particular relevance here was the person's sense of control (carried out by Margie E. Lachman and Suzanne L. Weaver of Brandeis University, 1998). Ages which ranged from 29 to 75 years of age, were divided into three age categories for comparative purposes: *young* (25-39 years of age), *middle-aged* (40-54 years of age) and an *older adult group* (ages 60-75). For those over 75, we projected results based on the MacArthur Study findings and other studies that focused on the 75 and over age category. Past studies and generally held societal beliefs have suggested that:

1) The perceived *control over life* was generally higher in middle age (40-54 years of age) than for either younger or older adulthood.[3] Many factors contributed to these beliefs including being at the peak of one's career, amassing financial resources, power exercised in business and institutional areas and mastering of family responsibilities.

2) *In health matters,* control over health was thought to decrease with age. It has been widely believed that the "natural" impairment of bodily functions and the senses added up to loss of control. Earlier studies confirmed this.[4] Current studies challenge the inevitability of some of these aging consequences!

Overall research results from the MacArthur study suggest that people have a relatively high sense of control in a general sense of "mastery" and in health-related matters, *irrespective of age.* Health was rated even higher than a "general sense of mastery", because the latter included many different factors involving such things as sexual relationships, work, financial security, marriage and finances.

The results in the health domain of the study signalled the need for *critically examining long-held beliefs often viewed as common knowledge!* Health measures went much beyond individual "impressions". Seven measures of physical health were obtained. Additional health-related items assessed risk related to cancer and heart attack, experiencing (recently) of 28 health-related problems and nine physical health/functionally related problems and symptoms. Although the (optimistic) research results for the over-75 years of age groups have been expected to change (i.e. decrease) for both general mastery and health, we may be in for some surprises here as well. Deepak Chopra (1993)[5] is among a number of medical and social scientists referencing specific studies of the 75 and over category. Others are cited at various points in these writings. The widespread and fast growing attention to these matters backed up by research and powerful communications capabilities, computers especially, promise a much more rapid dissemination of information than that experienced in the past. Both research and application will benefit greatly from these advances.

A HEALTH REVOLUTION AND
NEW HEALTH CARE ROLES

The revolution in the delivery of health care and medical services since the 1960's means that individuals must now assume an unprecedented role in managing their own health. The fast growth of HMO's, PPO's and group practices and the demise of individual practice are now signs of the times familiar to most all. Growing national awareness of out-of-control health costs, tighter monitoring of health agencies, and stricter limitations on health care fees, have resulted in a growing emphasis on out-patient services, faster turn-over of hospital beds and medical personnel exercising time management in connection with patients. Arguably some of these are the positive results of attempting to moderate out-of-control medical costs and to extend at least minimal health care services to many more people. But what has not been recognized is that literally millions of people have not been prepared for the new roles they must assume in consequence of these changes. For example, the explosion of health-related research results have virtually buried us in information. Many feel overwhelmed regardless of age.

Depersonalization of doctor-patient relationships is another part of the picture. Doctor-patient relationships are increasingly mediated by lack of time, periodic personnel shortages and dependence on computer and phone technology. A little-discussed point is the fact that patient medical files can become voluminous after years of treatment. Yet the time demands on medical personnel makes it ever more difficult to critically assess records of treatment, let alone work out future health maintenance strategies for the person. Adding to these problems is the fact that the huge number of *aging baby boomers* who now "feel great and years younger than their age," will be increasingly in need of medical/health services. Compounding the health care delivery is the fact that many are not pursuing the lifestyles and taking the steps needed for better health quality assurance in their "senior" years.[6] Many lack preparation or are misinformed.

In the aging society, one should also be wary of the need to change the mindset of many individuals to one that is much more *proactive* regarding their health and well being. Advances in medical technology, pharmacology and health care delivery have contributed significantly to advances in longevity and quality of life. That's the good news! However, these achievements may also give a false sense of security or send out the wrong message. The thrust of many of these advances has stressed *technology-based* health care strategies and politically neutral (safe) environmental monitoring (e.g., air, water quality) approaches. The societal aspects of these developments are so important that they are further discussed in a later section.

No doubt, the medical profession would strongly endorse a proactive approach by the person yet they are in an increasingly constrained position due in part to factors previously mentioned. Also, a notable point is that many of the advances and the information related to healthier lifestyles, especially in recent years, emerged largely outside of the traditional medical establishment! Some 60 percent of people recently surveyed claim that they have used non-traditional health approaches in the last few years. Examples of these would include acupuncture, herb therapies, vegetarian diets, Tai Chi and meditation. Many medical practitioners justifiably claim that the benefits of many of these therapies and lifestyle changes are as yet to be *scientifically* validated. Yet, literally millions of people now believe that these approaches are helping them achieve a better quality of life or that they just simply feel better. They assume a more positive attitude regarding their lives, health and possibilities. There is no doubt that attitudes are powerful factors in wellness and recovery. Additionally, it is of interest to note that there are a growing number of medical profession members who are now starting to contribute to this new-era technology and literature. For example, Michael F. Roizen (1999), James S. Gordon (1996), Herbert Benson (1975, 1986), John Rowe (1998), Bernie Siegel (1986), Deepak Chopra (1993), Dean Ornish (1992) and Andrew Weil (1995)[7] are making an important impact in defining this field and validating newer approaches. Concepts of the scientific method are being exploited. Also, newer roles are being defined for the individual and medical practitioner in jointly achieving and maintaining good health.

Although knowledge precedes focused action, getting started to realize the benefits of a particular cause-effect relationship is hardly assured. Initiating personal change can be a daunting challenge. Many aging boomers and seniors, say, those 55 to 80 years of age, have not moved into healthful behavior patterns even where there is an awareness of quality of life and longevity possibilities! In the large scale Mid-life Study (1999)[8], sponsored by the prestigious MacArthur Foundation, it was found that among those in the 40 to 75 years of age range, many had *not* enacted the lifestyle changes required for fulfilling their QL (quality of life) and longevity possibilities. For more on this subject, see the chapter on Individual Change (IV-3).

The changes described thus far have been largely of a reactive-adaptive rather than proactive nature. Untold millions have been faced with rapid health care related challenges and in some cases, the need for fast change in life threatening situations. Many have been doing their best to cope or adapt. But we would be remiss if we did not acknowledge equally compelling developments leading to the creation of a "new" medicine built on new assumptions and patient-doctor (health care deliverer)

relationships.[9]
Creating a "New" Medicine

A newer multifaceted synthesis is taking place in creating the "new" medicine. It is built on a foundation combining ancient and modern sources that are both conventional and unusual. It includes findings from the best of modern science yet also incorporates durable aspects of (traditional) medical wisdom.[10] It also envisions a new "partnership" involving the individual and medical practitioner.

The signs are growing that a "new" medicine is being defined involving both medical practitioners and individuals. For medical personnel it means taking a broader view of medicine, healing and being human.[11] It also means looking at people holistically; biologically, physically, psychologically and perhaps spiritually too. Many younger people entering the health care profession and growing numbers of seasoned medical practitioners are helping to define a new therapeutic relationship. The fact that far more people are aware and informed regarding health matters, *suggests an egalitarian* rather than authoritarian relationship. It is one in which *both* the practitioner and individual must meet the *qualifying assumptions* of the new health orientation. Vital ingredients include exercise, nutrition and diet, meditation, relaxation and self-awareness built on a solid foundation of holistic thinking about health matters. Mind, body and spirit are inexorably woven together; more on this shortly.

The new health orientation acknowledges that optimal health results require promoting good health as a way of life. The person is expected to bring to the relationship a new level of being informed regarding general health matters and self-awareness that combines physical and psychological dimensions. The person knows about "biofeedback" *and* uses it to maintain and improve his/her health. Also the person seeks to continually improve their knowledge and skills through study, meditation and various biofeedback techniques. Another feature is that both the medical person and individual project an optimistic, hopeful attitude towards healthful living and the experiencing of illness. In some cases, it may mean that the "medical person" is one licensed and educated in the less well known but viable areas of the current medical profession. It may also mean newer, important and growing areas such as acupuncture, massage and aroma therapy, and nutritionists with both western and eastern training. Arguably, these are controversial areas but irreversible changes are already taking place in these areas. It also means that even death can be contemplated in a useful, comforting framework of "life completion".[12] Clearly, many will not be able to or choose not to engage in this new relationship but now at least we have a model of possibilities.

THERAPIES FOR THE HEALTH INFORMATION EXPLOSION

Although health-related information seems to be coming at us from all directions, we have found that in the main, much of it sorts out into three related but recognizably different areas. These are: *research results* generated by health, medical and social scientists and first reported in the literature of their fields; *practitioner syntheses* based on widespread knowledge, experiences and readings of health and medical practitioners, scientists and reputable consultants from various fields; and *precepts* drawn from the *world's great religions, belief and way-of-life systems*. In theory, these are rather distinct identifiable categories; in reality, the boundaries blur rapidly. They are, however, a useful point of departure, no more but no less. Each is discussed briefly in this section though their general importance goes much beyond these limited remarks.

Part of the essential knowledge base for health self-management involves critically examining information sources and assumptions. For our purposes, all are considered as a part of a comprehensive framework of mind-body-spirit approaches and a schema for understanding your own attitudes.

Research: Sorting Things Out

As a matter of experience, prestigious news sources provide one benchmark for judging timeliness, relevance and authenticity. These include, but are not limited to, the *New England Journal of Medicine* and "health letters" from recognized sources such as the Mayo Clinic, Johns Hopkins University, the University of California at Berkeley, the Harvard Medical School , Dr. Andrew Weil's "Self Healing", Mt. Siani Hospital, and the Center for Science in the Public Interest. Highly reputable editors and review boards sift through hundreds of findings, discoveries and reports to identify timely and what appears to be solid information, *as of that particular point in time!* Have they ever provided information that turns out to be highly unreliable? Yes! But the probabilities of bad information are generally quite low and they have good, long-term track records. As an aside, the bases for grading the reliability of these sources are very similar to those in the financial field for investment purposes. The "test" of common sense is often an additional criterion but counter-intuitive findings and *whose* common sense is being used are realities we need to face. For example, it is widely known that antibiotics kill bacteria. Thus, *if* they work, lives may be saved. But if cattle or pigs have been routinely fed antibiotics to stimulate their growth, the immunity of various bacteria strains is increased.[13] If you or a family member is fighting an infection caused by one of these bacteria strains, your doctor's prescription may be of little help, even useless. However, even the health news from (relatively) reliable sources must be carefully read and digested. A case in point concerns the fiber story. For years, health specialists, practitioners, foundations and publications idealized high-fiber diets to head off colon cancer. The "fine print" often forgotten was that fiber also contributed to regularity and the possibility that high fiber diet people had lowered their risk of several major diseases.[14] Thus, even if the last word was not in yet on fiber and colon cancer, its other benefits likely justified its continuing importance in the diet. Yet, when one of the Harvard Medical School researchers released data (January 1999) from the huge, long-term "Nurses' Health Study" of no linkage between cancer and fiber, newspapers, TV and radio reports headlined the news. Forgotten were the other beneficial effects. All kinds of health "mavens" suddenly justified gross diets of sweets, fats and cutting back on fruits and vegetables!

Types of Research

Research studies tend to fall into four broad categories: retrospective; cross-sectional; prospective; and clinical trials. Advantages of getting results fairly quickly *(retrospective and cross-sectional)* must be weighed against lack of detail and often quality (usually provided in *prospective studies and clinical trials*). Also, the number of people for whom results are being reported figures importantly into the authenticity of results. In prospective studies researchers track large groups over a period of five, ten or more years. If the *prospective study* starts with a relatively healthy group, the focus may then center on who gets particular diseases and how diets, age or lifestyle affect the incidence of a particular disease. Once the group (and thereby geographic area) has been selected, the information reported is the information used. Since different cultural groups have tended to settle in different areas and climactic differences are another geographic fact, "area" per se may be a major variable! No attempt is made by the researchers in the prospective study to influence lifestyles, diets or setting. Some prospective studies involve thousands of participants as for example, the Harvard Female Nurses' Study (120,000), Harvard's Health Professionals Follow-up Study (40,000), the Iowa Women's Health Study (29,000) and the Framingham (Massachusetts) Heart Study (6,000). The fact that data are (often) collected at successive points over time reduces the problems of forgetfulness and recall experienced in a *retrospective study.*

In *cross-sectional studies*, a snapshot is taken at a point in time. The cross-sectional data emphasize inter-comparisons of individuals or groups across geographic, age, institutional and/or health boundaries. Some of these studies are also called retrospective if participants need to recall past incidents, diets, lifestyles and/or critical incidents. The relative speed with which data are generated must be weighed against recall issues and frequent lack of preciseness.

Clinical trials, a key argument used by medical purists, usually provide a high degree of control though they may not generate data for years. This is a highly controversial area. Results may be disappointing, though much time has passed and great effort and money expended. The research methodology may have been OK, but the original hypotheses or logic guiding the study may have turned out to be faulty. Of course sometimes that is the only way growth occurs; knowing what is wrong as well as what is right! Though expensive and time-consuming, their precision and control is often compelling. It appears that the populations of advanced countries have crossed a critical threshold of acceptance for clinical trial approaches. Arguably, it appears to be the only way to go for many in a highly complex, dynamic society, and they are increasing. Yet, their cost and time, especially where life-threatening diseases are involved, have generated a growing debate in this area.

In the clinical trial, individuals are randomly assigned to groups and then one group receives a special diet or the like while the other one gets or maintains an ordinary diet. After several years the groups are compared as to the incidence of particular problems, health states or diseases.

At first glance, "research" may appear far removed from the interest or possible understanding of the health consumer. Yet, a *working knowledge* of health research basics is critical to the individuals who have never been put into the driver's seat of managing their own health!

There are many words and terms that have come into common use regarding aging but few have considered their real impact in the aging society. Older, old, aging, real age and middle age are a modest representation of these. In the next chapter, we set out a concept of "quality age" (QA) as a reasonable approximation of one's robustness. It is an approximation of a person's real age that incorporates physiological, biological and psychological features. Chronological age is relegated to a secondary position, an often poor guide to one's quality of life and length of life expectations.

Chapter II – 2

How Old Are You Really?
Quality Age

HOW OLD ARE YOU REALLY?

People who live healthier

live longer and with less

disease and disability

Michael F. Roizen[1]

HOW OLD ARE YOU?
PSYCHOLOGICAL DIMENSIONS

How old are you really? Forty or fifty years ago this question could have been readily answered based on chronological age, albeit, it was not voluntarily communicated by many. Most of the time it was like a fishing expedition, if you dared to ask the question "How old are you?". For Baby Boomers sliding past 50, you might get an evasive response: "Oh, I don't know. We don't make a big deal out of birthdays anymore." In our youth oriented culture, telling one's real age was like an admission of guilt, especially for those past 60 and still working. An anecdote from our teaching days further clarifies this point. At retreats, a favorite meeting "ice breaker" was to ask all members of a particular age cohort to raise their hands, gather in a corner of the meeting room to share experiences and then report back to the reassembled group. Strangely, by the time individuals reached their late 50's and 60's, virtually nobody raised their hands – at least high enough to make them generally visible. Over the years, several of us "seniors" started to (more) carefully observe who was responding. We knew a rather large circle of people including their actual or approximate (chronological) age. Many near or past their mid 50's simply weren't playing the game. At a subsequent meeting, one of the featured workshops focused on issues confronting aging academics. It became clear that many academics greatly played down their own age and even aging issues. Older was generally considered old, and thus out of touch, not better nor wiser. Older members were gradually worked out of the power structure and were less and less frequently sought out for advice. Similar patterns were common in the general business scene. Thus, even though a factual base existed for the question "How old are you?", it was an infrequent topic for general discussion. It was even greatly limited in social circles albeit unless it was a "revelation" about "such and such's" age. The general tone of our youth oriented society was one of age-ism. It was amply attested to by the number of complaints brought under Federal age discrimination legislation.

Now, however, this situation is starting to change and quite rapidly. The explosion in health related research, fast growing interests in health matters, deepening penetration of the aging society and newer concepts driving home longevity and quality of life (QL) possibilities, have all been factors. Needless to say, a cohort of 70 million Baby Boomers crossing into "middle age" has served as a compelling factor to re-examine these matters. For our purposes, "age" has taken on multiple dimensions. Of particular interest in this chapter is "quality age" which we have referred to in past discussions as comprising both psychological and physical or biological dimensions.

UNCOMMON COMMON KNOWLEDGE

It used to be "common knowledge" that once people moved into middle age, they simply started to "wear out". Hair thinned, endurance lessened, memory started to go and various other measures of robustness started to decline. Some have likened the experience to the old style 6-volt battery systems. The battery would start out with a full charge but then gradually decline. Replacement time was a judgment call and replacement life often (it seemed) a poor guess. The worst was "suddenly" one cold morning when we couldn't start the car (see EXHIBIT A-A). We

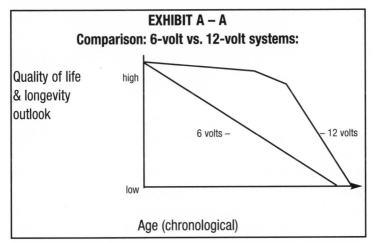

EXHIBIT A – A
Comparison: 6-volt vs. 12-volt systems:

Quality of life & longevity outlook

high

6 volts –

– 12 volts

low

Age (chronological)

accepted the inevitability of this situation because "that was the way things were".

The introduction of the 12-volt systems changed all that (EXHIBIT A-A). They had a higher, more consistent output for most of their life, greater reliability and a longer life. The differences are more apparent when the 12-volt performance curve is superimposed upon that of the 6-volt (EXHIBIT A-A). Performance and length of life differences are brought out more dramatically. "Which would you prefer?" Despite the obvious superiority of the 12-volt system, old habits and beliefs die hard. When newer 12-volt systems with improved performance (EXHIBIT A-A) were introduced, many still clung to maintenance, performance and replacement thinking characteristic of the old rather than the new systems. Deeply rooted experiences had been transformed into beliefs and expectations that were difficult to change despite the demonstrated superior output and longer life of the new systems. This situation is not unlike that encountered in health care, and longevity and quality of life thinking.

Ideas of aging and decline become deeply rooted in the human psyche. Thus, the rather remarkable demographic trends and health related movements of the last few decades went largely unnoticed by the general public, though they were already being hotly contested in professional circles.

For better than two decades the "evidence" has grown that we were in the midst of a multi-dimensional longevity revolution without precedent.[2] As the news slowly spread, the expectation of living longer than our parents or previous generations was in and of itself a rather remarkable revelation. Now add to this picture the fact that *most people also had the ability to substantially change the quality of their lives as well!*

Natural aging tendencies affecting the resilience and plasticity of individuals can often be delayed, neutralized, or at times even reversed.[3] Truly we are entering a newer, fast emerging world loaded with exciting possibilities for individual living and enjoyment. The "catch" is that most all of us will have to get more deeply involved in our own health matters. There will be much new to learn and experience as new behavior patterns.

AGING, NEW PERSPECTIVES

We are having to re-calibrate most all of our traditional aging definitions, measures and ideas as knowledge related to wellness and longevity exploded. Social scientists would hasten to say that the definitions must be embedded in social and cultural phenomena – our national ethos. We need only to look about us and note that "he/she doesn't look like his/her age". Newspapers daily carry stories about the 75 or 80 year old who ran in the "5K", or the woman who had a child at 60 years of age, or the Baby Boomer who launched a second or third career at age 55. With good reason we ask "What is *youth?*", "What is *aging* and what are the signs of aging?" and "Who is *old?*". At the end of the 19ᵗʰ century, the social ethos was "sloughing off the aged (old) in society and embracing the promise of society's youth".

The social meaning of age has been changing.[4] At one time, the major life marker for "middle age" was children growing up and leaving the parental home. Work and working dominated our life roles. Old age was the time immediately preceding and following retirement from work. It was usually marked by "rapidly declining physical and intellectual vigor, chronic illness, social disengagement" and often by isolation and desolation.[5] This is now changing radically.

The blurring of middle age and old age distinctions have been signaled by the growth in terms such as "young-old" and "old-old", meaning, respectively, healthy and vigorous though up in years, and declining physical and intellectual vigor and disengagement, with aging. It is worthy of note that even in some of the oldest age cohorts, say those above 85, more than one-third report no limitations due to age![6] Truly the rhythm of life cycle distinctions has been so distorted that we can seriously question their utility. A new "second adulthood" is upon us, but it raises some realistic challenges.

One of the surprising results from a ten-year long study (MacArthur Foundation, 1998)[7] involving thousands of individuals from 40 to 75 years of age, was that people on the average felt almost eleven years younger than their chronological age! Psychologically, this was wonderful news! However, gerontologists are not easily put off by good intentions or a positive life outlook. They confront people with the central challenge, "Are you prepared to pursue the life style and health practices which will validate your potential for feeling good and longevity now accessible to so many?"

THE NEW SECOND ADULTHOOD

The possibilities for a "new second adulthood"[8] were born out of the stretching out of average life span, economic trends and remarkable health and medical advances. Clarification of the economic – financial issues is addressed in a subsequent chapter. Clarification of some of the key health and longevity related issues are considered here. These include several interrelated questions:

1. "If indeed a new second adulthood is emerging, then what are its assumptions or contingencies?"
2. "What are the dimensions or characteristics of the second adulthood paradigm? How are we to think about chronological age?"
3. "What in effect is our 'real age'?"

Although many have credited Baby Boomers with being the leading edge of societal change to a new plateau of quality living and longevity, they are more accurately seen as the beneficiaries of previous generational contributions.[9] World War II and depression age cohorts established tentative models of quality of life and longevity possibilities. They also sparked health science, philosophical and gerontological initiatives which were admittedly self-serving but also facilitated a rapid health transformation in the Boomer's group. Thus, Baby Boomers were the first generation to fully benefit from life extending advances in the medical and health sciences and technology. Additionally, the sheer size of the Baby Boomer's cohort possessed the numbers (some 70 million) to achieve a critical mass for *self-sustaining change.* This force could energize a major societal transformation in health related thinking, quality of life and longevity. Of course there isn't much point in talking about this new *theory* of a "second adulthood" unless 1) there is a good chance of getting there, and 2) once arrived, enjoying most of the experience. If one is already in this age range, one's interest shifts towards, "Can I still achieve longevity and quality of life benefits from making healthful changes?" and/or "How do I maximize my experiences and possibilities?"

Another Look at the "Second Adulthood"

The following discussions deal with some of the main issues related to the three questions posed at the start of this section. The first regarding assumptions and contingencies has already been addressed. The others will require a much more extensive development. Longevity is a double-edged sword. It is potentially both a blessing and a curse. If we live more years but lose independence and feel poorly most of the time, or are "out of it" most of the time, many would take a pass on the extra years. On the other hand, if the extra years were largely blissful, a time to catch up, to do some of the things they always wanted to do, to give back to society some of the time, attention and wisdom they have enjoyed, most would wholeheartedly welcome the extension of their lives. For sure there are no guarantees when it comes to longevity and quality of living for a particular individual. But, as already established in the chapter "You Bet Your Life", the odds strongly favor achieving many of these possibilities if we are prepared to change, or more particularly, move into healthful living patterns.

The next chapter focuses in on some particulars in this area.

Chapter II – 3

Characteristics of "Second Adulthood People": A Newer View of Age and Aging

CHARACTERISTICS OF "SECOND ADULTHOOD PEOPLE": A NEWER VIEW OF AGE AND AGING

Background

Chronological age has proven to be increasingly inadequate as a predictor of longevity and an individual's state of health. Advances in health technology and nutritional and brain-body knowledge and research have taken place at such an astonishing rate as to undercut the utility of chronological age in these matters. Chronological age still has an important role to play but inferences regarding longevity and quality of life must be greatly augmented with much other information. Thus, health and social scientists have, as mentioned previously, come up with such terms as "young-old" and "old-old" to indicate the relative vitality of a person who is old chronologically. These terms, too, have their obvious limitations.

We have found it useful to think of age in several dimensions. "New Age" thinking has championed a holistic approach to individuals which includes mind, body and spirit. From a large body of "New Age" literature[1], we have culled out two dimensions of age and some other descriptions which have proven useful in describing older (say 50+) population segments. These are 1) chronological (CA), and 2) biological or physical condition (BA). In addition, a person's mental health (the "psychological" aspects) and "emotional intelligence" for example, would serve as important descriptions of overall quality of life and individual adaptation and coping ("functionality"). An overall age descriptive term summarizing these many factors would, aside from chronological age, be "quality age".

By biological or physical age we include such elements as blood pressure, functions of the heart and the immune and respiratory systems, hearing and visual acuity and strength and endurance. Also, "psychological age", if we were to use this term, would refer to one's general mental health and brain functioning. Brain functioning includes rapidity of decision making, short-term memory and mental/situational adaptability to fast changing situations. Also, a youthful rather than stodgy outlook and one that optimistically includes health-longevity matters. All of these tend to favor a youthful perspective. This suggests one who has the ability to fully participate in and enjoy their unfolding life experiences.

Other Factors Making the Whole Individual

In addition to these two primary age dimensions there is also a type of emotional sophistication and wisdom that must also be considered. Since the idea of an "emotional age" moves counter to conventional thinking, the term is used sparingly in our discussions. Daniel Goleman[2] advanced the highly useful concept of "Emotional Intelligence" to cover various mental abilities which his research indicated were a far better predictor of an individual's work/business/social success than the traditional I. Q. (intelligence quotient). The concept is relevant to our discussion of longevity and quality of living because it provides insights as to one's wisdom, maturity in decision making, and one's success in social situations. All of these are bound to affect one's quality of living experiences and perhaps longevity as well.

Another idea related to quality of life is that of wisdom, the ability to artfully draw from one's experiences. Up to a point at least, "wisdom" should improve with age though unfortunately many of us may know of some (many?) exceptions to this "rule". Others only half-jokingly say that some aging people even seem to get "crotchety" and less willing to accept change in their own lives. Thus, in any realistic assessment of a particular individual's quality of life (existence), factors related to the person's emotional intelligence and maturity (wisdom) would have to be included. Thus, the two age dimensions, chronological and biological-physical represent only an initial approximation of one's actual situation. Also, it is quite well established that a person's mental state and emotional maturity affect such things as stress and adaptability and thus impact biological-physical processes, eg., heart, blood pressure, and immune system functioning.

LOOKING AT AGE IN THREE DIMENSIONS

Perhaps the single most important point is that the two age dimensions (chronological and biological-physical) represent different ways of looking at the same person. In addition, let's consolidate the other factors and for convenience, call these "psychological age". To an important extent, two of the three may then reflect personal choices or factors which the individual can influence! Chronological age (CA) is a "given", but psychological age (PA) and biological age (BA) can be importantly, maybe greatly, influenced by the person. Consequently, there is every reason to believe that PA and BA represent numerous and different combinations in connection with CA.

The following example and scenario suggest how these three age dimensions could be used in a practical way. These illustrations and discussions are followed by a discussion of some particular ways that an individual can develop strategies for improving quality of life and longevity possibilities.

THE AGE GAME

As one moves into the "second adulthood" years (50+ years of age), numerous and different combinations of these factors become possible.

Consider the following:

1. Baby Boomers, whose chronological age is 50 years:
   a. Psychological Age – 40, Biological Age – 50
   b. Psychological Age – 50, Biological Age – 40
   c. Psychological Age – 60, Biological Age – 55
   d. Psychological Age – 50, Biological Age – 50
2. Some "Seniors", whose chronological age is 65 years:
   a. Psychological Age – 50, Biological Age – 50
   b. Psychological Age – 65, Biological Age – 50
   c. Psychological Age – 75, Biological Age – 70
   d. Psychological Age – 65, Biological Age – 65

Let's consider several of these combinations as typical of the range of situations to be found in "real life":

- Baby Boomers (chronological age of 50); psychological age = 40 and biological age = 50 (1a). This person's outlook is positive and relatively optimistic regarding life's possibilities and what the future will bring. She continues to find life stimulating and interesting. At the same time, though still physically active, she has started to cut back a bit on workouts, long walks and the like. Perhaps she is caught up in the professional demands of her job.

- Baby Boomers (chronological age of 50); psychological age = 60 and biological age = 55 (1c). This Boomer has gone through much at work and in his family life. Corporate downsizings have led to a succession of jobs and the family has been forced to relocate several times. An earlier failure to connect in his first marriage led to a divorce, remarriage and now a new family dynamic with his children and her children too. Although he used to have a regular tennis game and worked out regularly at the "club", loss of jobs due to the downsizings forced him to drop these stress relievers.

- Senior (chronological age of 65); psychological age = 50 and biological age = 50 (2a). This person has kept himself in good physical condition through daily walks, aerobics, and a modified vegetarian diet. He says that with lifestyle changes, especially in his eating habits, he feels better, is more alert and feels in control of his situation. Thus, it is no surprise that (psychologically) he is optimistic about pursuing his options and living each day to the fullest.

- Senior (chronological age of 65); psychological age = 75 and biological age = 70 (2c). Her husband passed away unexpectedly when she was only 55 years of age. She never remarried. Fortunately she had a small circle of friends from years ago with whom she regularly played bridge. Although her children nagged her for years about "some exercise and cutting back on the carbs and sweets," it always seemed disruptive to her lifestyle. Although she has regularly attended "lifetime learning" sessions with health content and even participated in a program of the "Weight Watchers," none of the possible lifestyle changes proved to be durable. She returned to her old habits.

Measuring "PA" and "BA"

"PA" and "BA" have been described in order to broaden individual outlooks regarding their quality of life and longevity possibilities. At this point no method exists to precisely measure these factors and perhaps none is needed if the import of these concepts is clear. For those who want a specific numbers-oriented approach, the excellent book by Michael Roizen (1999), *Real Age*[3] is recommended. More related ideas are provided in the following chapter.

Nature-Nurture Revisited: A Concluding Note

"You don't get something for nothing" rings practically true when it comes to longevity and quality of life matters. Aside from the fortunate few who draw on strong gene pools and "stumble" through the "disease minefield", most people will have to modify to varying degrees, long-standing health and lifestyle practices. The good news is that moving into the longevity-quality of life mode can take place at most anytime in one's life. Clearly, the sooner one moves into the newer lifestyle patterns, the quicker the health returns and the greater the long-term effects. There are no guarantees in the game of healthful living but the odds will (heavily) favor the person who makes these choices.

The next chapter on Quality Age provides ingredients for health strategies and some information on how more specific descriptive and numerical analyses may be undertaken regarding quality of life-longevity possibilities.

PART III

Mapping Health Success Strategies

Chapter III – 1

Mapping Health Success Strategies: Background

MAPPING HEALTH SUCCESS STRATEGIES: BACKGROUND

The central theme underlying PART III is that many, perhaps most people, can importantly affect both their quality of living (QL) and longevity! Further, we are assuming that increased longevity without maintaining a reasonable semblance of quality living is unacceptable. Thus, in all our discussions QL and increased longevity go hand in hand. The person at 70 years of age may not be able to do what he/she did at 40 years of age, but he/she can potentially achieve functional activities and quality living patterns among the better or best of one's age cohort. In this sense the "Quality Age" for a person at birthday number 60 may be significantly better than that of a friend celebrating 50.

People can make *choices* that can affect both their QL and longevity! A decision to live more healthfully is the first step in a process focused on a person living longer, and at a level of vitality and energy often thought to be the exclusive province of the young. Obviously, there are no guarantees but we can move in the direction with the greatest likelihood of successful outcomes. A decision to live more healthfully means that the person is increasingly in a position to reduce his/her vulnerability to diseases and disabilities.

As brought out at various points in the previous discussions, one's family history (the "genes") still have an important role to play in both QL and longevity. But the good news is that it is a role much diminished over that in the past. For example, the "genes" accounted for some 70 percent to 80 percent of one's predictable QL and longevity in the past. The corresponding figure today might be 20 percent to 30 percent if thoughtful living and health patterns are followed. Naturally, the exact amount is arguable but these percentages communicate the sense of the enormous changes (advances) that have taken place in health-related technologies and processes. Traditional medical and health approaches have been augmented with many new and powerful "allies".

Another breakthrough idea is that a decision to live and launch a more healthful living pattern can be made at most any point in a person's life and with some attendant benefits ultimately resulting. Short of angelic or heavenly interventions, there is nevertheless much the person can do to affect both QL and longevity. In years gone by there were only a modest number of research studies focused on QL and longevity experiments. One example would be results proclaiming "notable improvements" for 80+ seniors in rest homes undertaking muscle-strengthening exercises.

Now "notable improvements" are routinely reported and achieved in a variety of studies. There is no question that the earlier in one's life that a healthful living program is launched, the greater the long-term benefits. However, the reality is that people came to a need and desire for more healthful living at various points in their lives. Many of the time differences in start-up reflect: the "fits and starts" of health innovations; changes in one's work or personal situation; the inertia of established health practices; as well as health-related institutions resisting major changes in these. Of equal importance in matters of health success programming are issues of individual motivation, especially where important lifestyle changes are required. This is discussed in a subsequent section.

The final introductory note is that mind, body and spirit (MBS), the pillars of "new age" thinking, initially represent equally viable points of entry into healthful lifestyles. What one feels comfortable with initially (M, B, or S) is the preferred point of entry for that person. The focus is a healthful living program and a basis for mapping corresponding health strategies. Eventually, if the person sticks with the desire for an improved, healthful lifestyle, the positive consequences of these will most likely encourage undertaking a more comprehensive strategy involving other MBS elements. It is at the point where MBS approaches are jointly undertaken that the synergy from these will bring notable results for the individual. The six key points underlying an initial approach to mapping health success strategies are summarized in EXHIBIT D-D.

There is little doubt that many myths surround individual limitations and the ability to change health and life patterns. The outpouring of anecdotal information and research study results are rapidly shattering these myths. The "mapping health success agenda" (EXHIBIT D-D) highlights some of the key developments in this area.

A Critical View of Individuals as Healthful Living Models

How do we select paradigms, tools or individuals as models of exemplary people representing healthful living practices? One group of approaches in recent years has been to identify those who have lived the longest, namely elder seniors or even centenarians. A few of these studies concentrated exclusively on centenarians as in the well-known New England Centenarian Study.[1]

EXHIBIT III: D-D
Longevity and Quality of Living (QL): An Agenda for Mapping Health Success Strategies

1. Most people can importantly affect both their QL and longevity.
2. People living healthfully live longer; they lessen their vulnerability to disease and disabilities.
3. Improved QL often means a higher level of energy and sense of vitality.
4. Genes or family history are still important to both longevity and QL but for many, are playing a smaller role today than in the past. In the future they are likely to play an even smaller role.
5. The decision to start living more healthfully can be made at most any age and some benefits reaped; naturally, the earlier the start, the greater the long-term benefits.
6. Mind-body-spirit represent alternate and initial entry points into a comprehensive, healthful living program. See the sketch that follows.

Pictorially, these three factors (point No. 6) can be represented as follows:

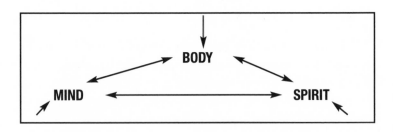

Next, "candidates" were further qualified on the basis of those who seemed to be experiencing a reasonable quality of life as well. Common factors were then searched out in the lives of these people and composite lists developed. In some studies, "longevity lists" were compiled statistically, permitting some factors to be weighted more heavily than others, or even negatively, so that a composite result could be determined.

These groups of factors have been highly useful in providing general lifestyle and behavioral guidelines. Also, identification of these factors have helped to focus additional research inquiries into these factors and underlying biological and longevity processes.

Aging, however, is not easily defined in biological terms. Leonard Hayflick, Ph.D., Professor of Anatomy at the University of California, San Francisco, has been quoted as saying that: "Aging is not merely the passage of time. It is the manifestation of biological events that occur over a span of time."[2]

Everybody's biological clock "ticks at a different rate" so that general health success factors should not be expected to impact a given person exactly the same way as in the success model's group. For example, some centenarians have smoked much of their lives yet virtually every medical study considers this a serious health/longevity threat!

Another point to be brought out has to do with the relative effects of one's genes, that is, the longevity, health history and quality of life experiences of an individual's parents and close relatives. Older seniors or centenarian groups typically assign high importance or weight these heavily in longevity determinations. Indeed their importance has been clearly established but as pointed out in a number of past discussions, dynamic health-related discoveries and applications have now shown the importance of newer approaches and processes largely outside of centenarian life experiences. Older seniors who are aware of and have practiced these newer approaches, experienced them at a relatively advanced life stage.

In short, it is our view that as additional age cohorts (especially the Baby Boomers) move past the 50 years of age marker, newer aging and health-related research and applications will have an increasing, perhaps dramatic impact on longevity and QL.

Chapter III – 2

Mapping Health Success Strategies: Methods

MAPPING HEALTH SUCCESS STRATEGIES: ALTERNATE APPROACHES

People differ widely in their learning styles, reflecting both personal preferences and aptitudes. Individual differences range from preferences for abstract reasoning to pragmatic, hands-on abilities and processes. Thus, we have erred on the side of presenting *multiple approaches* from which people can choose those which feel most comfortable for themselves. All the techniques described however, share a common theme; it is that they are comprehensive (mind, body and spirit) and are based on the assumptions summarized in Exhibit D-D.

Some of the approaches to be described seek to calculate the effects of various health-related practices and alternatives. These are similar to examples described in the last chapter. There, various combinations of chronological age and biological-physical age were discussed. Factually, no medically accepted technique exists for calculating a person's biological-physical age. At this stage of research, the numbers depict relative differences. However, medical researchers are coming ever closer to an accurate "Quality Age" determination for a particular person. Regardless of the underlying problems in making these calculations, the relative importance of these numerical approximations or even qualitative descriptive approaches, is not diminished.

"Vitality-Energy Scorecard"

A rich body of health-related "do's and don'ts" now exist. These represent the bountiful crop of rapid advances in health-related methods and processes. When viewed this way, they fall into several distinct categories which in total comprise the person's "health or vitality-energy scorecard". Dr. Michael De La Cruz is among the pioneers who has advocated this type of simple but powerful tool to facilitate individual diagnosis and improved health self-management. A format patterned after the work of De La Cruz[3] is displayed in EXHIBIT 2 F-F.

EXHIBIT III – 2 F-F

SUCCESS MAPPING: THE SCORECARD

Are you doing all you can do?
Being the person you want to be?

QUALITY AGE LEVEL

	Adding to	Subtracting from
MIND	1	4
BODY	2	5
SPIRIT	3	6

There are three features of the "Scorecard" which are important to note: 1) Mind, Body and Spirit (MBS) are all represented, 2) M, B and S have both positive (healthful, energy/vitality building) and negative (health detracting or lessening energy/vitality) activities, and 3) A person can work on any one of six options ("cells") at any particular time. That is, a person can seek to eliminate most negative items or attempt to add in more positive approaches to his/her lifestyle. This provides a flexible and fertile basis for longer-term "high scorecard" strategies. In short, the approach is to add thoughtfully (positively) to M, B and S and lessen those activities and habits detrimental to healthful living. This said, however, we are not depreciating the major motivational challenge these represent, a subject receiving much attention in a subsequent chapter.

BENCHMARKING AND FIRST THINGS FIRST

Before undertaking any suggested "scorecard" or "Quality Age" methods or processes, the individual will need to establish a profile of where they are today. A visit with a physician is an initial step and logical source of critical information. There is the need to establish safe parameters or boundaries within which the person can undertake exercise routines, shift food/nutritional patterns and the like. Clearly, no individual should initiate activities linked to health and the body's biological structure until he/she has *checked things out with his/her doctor.* Also, the physician will be a valuable source of biological and functional benchmarks including blood chemistry, lung capacity, functional abilities, bone density (especially for post-menopausal women!), etc. These types of readings/measurements will prove to be especially valuable since "scorecard"-related processes are likely to play out over an extended time interval. This point is closely linked to the whole process of individual adaptation to Mind-Body-Spirit changes.

launching of "Scorecard" or "Quality Age" techniques typically extends over many months and years. For example, EXHIBIT III – 2 G-G that follows, contains many activities either contributing to or detracting from one's state of health and sense of wellness. An individual program which, for example, incorporated many of the positive items could easily stretch out over several years. Why? Because the key to achieving longer-term benefits involves mind-body adaptations before a new, *stable* plateau of nutrition and lifestyle activities is achieved.

EXHIBIT III – 2 G-G

SCORECARD FACTORS

Positive Factors:

1) Mind
   - Mental exercise, challenges
   - Meditation
   - Relaxation Response (breathing)
   - Lifetime learning
   - Seeking "new age" behavior models
   - Stress consciousness
   - Inspirational readings   *...exhibit continues*

(EXHIBIT III-2 G-G continued)

2) Body
- Regular exercise
- Adequate, consistent sleep pattern
- Proper weight maintenance
- Nutrition-guided lifestyle
-· Breathing healthfully
- Body awareness/biofeedback savvy
- Strengthen, maintain relationships

3) Spirit
- Peace of mind, lifestyle, living guides
- Prayer and gratitude to higher being
- Love, loving
- Pursuit, practice of inspirational beliefs
- Mentoring, volunteering – giving back to the community
- Life-completion exercises when appropriate
- Forgiveness

Decreasing Negative Factors

4) Mind
- Minimizing contacts with pessimistic or unhappy people
- Avoid non-supportive, negative people
- Eliminate negative self-talk
- Reduce/eliminate exposure to violence
- Minimize mindless activity
- Decrease/eliminate grudges/being unforgiving
- Confront worry

...exhibit continues

(EXHIBIT III-2 G-G concluded)

5) Body
  - Reduce/eliminate junk foods
  - Reduce/eliminate smoking and all but moderate alcohol consumption
  - Critically review long-term drug consumption
  - Eliminate body-punishing sports, exercises
  - Critically review isolation producing activities

6) Spirit
  - Minimize contacts with non-believers
  - Give up belief myths
  - Critically examine religious avoidance pattern
  - Confront hate

SCORECARD METHODS AND PROCESSES

EXHIBIT III – 2 F-F provided a "scorecard" format. EXHIBIT 2 G-G provides over 40 activities and processes that can either add to or detract from healthful living patterns. We have culled these activities and processes from dozens of recent health/vitality/aging-related studies representing both traditional and non-traditional sources. A representative list of these is provided at the end of this chapter.

Applying a "Scorecard" Approach

For purposes of gaining some familiarity with health strategies based on a "Health Scorecard" approach, consider the following situations:

1. *A person relates readily to physical ("body")
approaches.* Being unfamiliar with health-related
processes, he has decided to do a self-audit of current
health-related activities with an eye to eliminating those
which are harmful. Since he is a non-smoker, this is no
problem, but alcohol consumption could be a problem. He
and his wife usually "knock off" a full bottle of wine for
dinner. Another rather obvious one is junk food snacking.
Since he spends much time in his car, he has had a habit of
keeping a large bag of snack food in the car. Whenever he
has gotten into heavy traffic, he takes out his bag of snacks
to help pass the time and not get aggravated. A
substitution of sugarless gum for the snack food and some
good tapes for his in-car tape player solved the eating-in-
the-car problem. A frank discussion between him and his
wife regarding wine consumption resulted in an agreement
to try out several different approaches; a) substitute some
non-alcoholic beverages and to reserve the wine-drinking
for going out, or b) stick with the wine but pour a glass of
wine for each and then remove the bottle from the table.

In order to get started on positive "Scorecard"
approaches, he decided to tackle several which seemed
comparatively easy. He checked out several health-related
books at the library. The approaches that he initially chose
were *healthful breathing* and more of a *nutrition-guided
lifestyle.* Another positive factor which captured his
attention was "breathing". Friends have often described to
him relaxation breathing. In the past, he dismissed these as
mostly over dinner or coffee break conversation pieces.
Seeing it appear in the "Scorecard List", he revisited the
area by dropping by a large bookstore near his house. Two
books caught his attention: Dr. Irwin Weil's (1999)
Breathing and Herbert Benson's (1994) *The Relaxation*

Response.[1] Together they provided solid information on breathing techniques and the potentially positive results from these. In a comparatively short period he was enjoying increasingly positive breathing results.

2. *A person elects "mental approaches" initially* as part of a general health strategy to keep her mind sharp. First she scans the negative factors and immediately finds two which she can relate to: "contacts with pessimistic or unhappy people" and "negative self-talk". For the first time she realized that two of her close friends seemed to constantly project "doom and gloom" or favor sedentary activities. Favorite discussion topics were the death of "such and such" and this one's cancer or that one's obesity. They seemed to have no interest in going to a healthful/wellness lecture (let alone a class!) or avoiding couch-potato activities; they could play bridge for an entire afternoon and several times a week.

Another self-discovery involved negative self-talk. She started keeping track of the number of times during the day or weekend that she blamed herself for her children's problems or self-expressed thoughts like "that's my stupidity" if she forgot something or something did not turn out as planned. Her "make-nice-to-me" program involved attending an Elderhostel program for the first time (!) where she met two nice people from her hometown and with whom she started to go out. Her scorecard method of assessing negative self-talk involved carrying a little card which she marked with time of day and thought every time she expressed a negative idea to herself. A friend suggested little notes for those things that seem to slip out of her mind. It turned out to be a practical solution for a long-standing problem and the extinguishing of an important source of negative thinking.

The "Scorecard" methods and processes just described represent a systematic way for the individual to start taking charge of health-longevity matters. The activities/factors described in EXHIBIT III–2 G-G provide numerous alternatives that an individual can first elect and then pursue. Some health researchers and gerontologists would likely feel that given the state of the art of health-longevity strategies for improving biological functioning, descriptive terms are perhaps as far as we should go. That is, avoid procedures that lead to rather concise numbers as estimates of our biological or "Quality Age" as opposed to the chronological age. Though having conviction, nevertheless some remarkable health/medical studies have turned up information and approaches to suggest that indeed, more systematic approaches may be possible. "Real Age", pioneered by Dr. Michael Roizen (1999)[2], is an outstanding example of one of these possibilities.

Chapter III – 3:

Mapping Health Success Strategies: Numerical Approaches (Part 1)

INTRODUCTION AND BACKGROUND:
THE MULTIPLE FACES OF AGE AND AGING

If you read Michael F. Roizen's 1999 national best seller *Real Age: Are You As Young As You Can Be?*[1], you are now likely aware of and perhaps convinced that your chronological age need not be the same as your biological age. Biologically, you may be years younger, equal to or years older than your chronological age. For the moment we will set aside the complications of "psychological age", or a related concept which has to do with the structural-skeletal and functional features of the person. "Biological age" is of great importance because it is directly linked to the person's quality of life and potential longevity as well.

Real Age presents a "revolutionary and systematic program for computing the aging effects of some 100 different health-related factors and behaviors".[2] Roizen and his scientific medical team truly brought about a defining moment in medicine; science research related to health, wellness and longevity. The team sifted carefully through over 25 years of research and writings representing some 25,000 studies. Roizen and his colleagues and their statistical support team modeled the impact on average life expectancy, of numerous health and medically related factors and behaviors. Their focus was one of determining the relative impact of these factors on a) longevity and b) quality of life (health, vigor and vitality). For those seeking a systematic assessment of these health and medically related factors and functions, on current outlooks and future expectations, this excellent resource is recommended. The reader's attention is also drawn to the discussion in the previous chapter, regarding the "scorecard" approach. This was one of several approaches we are presenting in order to provide various options for the reader.

In order to suggest some of the numerous and excellent insights brought about through a numerical type approach, we have developed the following scenario built around a real life incident. The setting for the situation is an annual picnic and outing for the "Mellon" family and some of their friends. It has been our experience that the implications of biologically related calculations or assertions are often brought home more graphically in a real life setting. The setting, calculations and inferences are those of the authors of this book and not in any way to be considered as provided or endorsed by Roizen and his associates.*

"LET'S HAVE A PICNIC":
AN APPLICATION EXAMPLE

Now, come join us at beautiful Ravinia Park in Highland Park, Illinois. Let's have a picnic and enjoy the wonderful music and beautiful setting.

The Mellon clan and friends gathered at Ravinia Park for their annual picnic. Younger family members were out at the park when it opened and raced in to stake out a favorably situated space. It had to be big enough to accommodate a possible 16 people including folding chairs, ice chests and picnic baskets. In the 25 years that the family and friends had been meeting at the park, many changes had taken place among the core Mellon family

---

* The examples and applications presented here are those of the authors and in no way should be considered as an example of Roizen's calculations.

members and friends. Marriages, births, divorces and deaths were part of the changes. Some friends and family members also had moved out of town and one Mellon family member now lived in Japan. Some of those moving out of town had gone down to South Florida and one couple went to Arizona. However, just a year after the Arizona couple moved into a Sun City development, the husband suddenly took ill and passed away. The wife, having had little time to make friends returned to Evanston, Illinois where she was able to rent a small apartment.

At the time of the picnic in late summer, the gathering reflected a full range of robust health and illness, part-time and full-time workers, and retirees. There were also married couples and single survivors -- all characteristics of older/mature individuals, families and their friends. Profiles of the 16 Mellon family members and their friends are summarized in EXHIBIT L-L and briefly described on next page.

EXHIBIT L-L provides name/social relationship, chronological age, "Quality Age" as it might have been calculated based on Roizen's type of information and methods[3], and lifestyle and/or current activities.

The following represents a brief summary of the information provided in EXHIBIT L-L:

a) The core of the Mellon family is represented by Father and Mother Mellon (#2) and the still living parents of Father Mellon (#1). They also have one son who is still living with them while attending graduate school (#3).

b) Cousins and friends, numbering ten (#5-#10) represent a full range of characteristic family

EXHIBIT L-L:
THE MELLON FAMILY AND FRIENDS

*CA = Chronological age

**"Quality Age" = based on factors such as those described by Roizen (1999), but also include such considerations as a person's sense of spirituality, continuing life challenge/ continuing education activity, etc. The examples are those of the authors and in no way should be considered as an example of Roizen's calculations.

NAME	CA*	Quality Age**	LIFESTYLE ACTIVITIES
1) Grandfather Mellon	83	86	Retired, uses wheelchair
Grandmother Mellon	80	75	Retired, tries to stay active
2) Father Mellon	53	53	Working, probably won't be able to retire. Has little time for exercise, etc.
Mother Mellon	50	42	Went back to work after last child finished college. Learned computers. "Having a ball". Very active.
3) Son	26	-	Goes to graduate school.
4) Richard (friend)	76	60	Divorced, "retired", robust, plays tennis regularly.
5) Harold and	73	80	Much overweight; just returned from
Dorothy (married)	73	-	Florida. Slim, active.
6) Helen and	78	75	Living together for companionship after
Bill (living together)	80	80	both lost spouses.
7) Howard and	72	55	Vegetarians, into volunteerism; active,
Ruth (married)	70	70	meditate regularly.
8) Larry and	87	80	Robust, part-time worker.
Margaret	82	79	Active, has maintained friendship circle.
9) Joan (widow)	78	70	Robust, active, good outlook on life.
10) Nancy (never married)	73	77	Much overweight.

situations ranging from spinsterhood (#10) to long-term marriage (#5 and #7) and older people living together (#6).

Of particular concern in this section on biological-chronological relationships, comparing the information regarding chronological age (column 2) and "Quality Age" (column 3) and the corresponding lifestyle/activity descriptions (column 4) are especially important.

c) Although Father and Mother Mellon are only three years different in chronological age (CA), their "Quality Age" (QA) differs by eleven years. At this point in their marriage the quality of life and longevity expectations of Mother Mellon are far more optimistic than those of her husband! If these differences were to continue in the future, Mother Mellon could anticipate many years of life without her mate. Correspondingly, Grandmother Mellon is doing much better than her husband (Grandfather Mellon). Clearly both Grandfather and Father Mellon could usefully pursue alternate health and medical strategies, at least based on initial assessment of their CA and QA calculations.

d) Friend Richard (#4) seems to be doing exceptionally well with his estimated QA, some sixteen years less than his CA. He continues to remain quite robust and still plays tennis regularly. His situation is similar to that of Howard (#7) and Joan (#9).

e) Lifestyle changes are clearly evident in the thumbnail sketch of "lifestyle activities". Howard and Ruth (#7) are vegetarians, Mother Mellon (#2) has re-entered schooling ("lifetime learning") and volunteerism and meditation (#7).

f) Overweight problems, often thought to be characteristic of many older people, plague Harold (#5), though his wife Dorothy is slim (!), as well as Nancy (#10).

g) Vigorous activities and robust lifestyles refute to the assumption that older people can't or don't choose to be this active (#'s 1, 2, 4, 5, 8, 9 and 10).

Chapter III – 4:

Mapping Health Success Strategies:
Numerical and Other Approaches, Part 2

INTRODUCTION

It has been our experience that familiarity with some preliminary, and somewhat broader assessments can greatly assist moving onto more detailed or numerical analyses. The "Scorecard" method described in Chapter III-2 was an example of a broader or descriptive approach. What follows, "Success Mapping", is built on a foundation of biologically related factors distilled from the work of various health/medical researchers and scientists. In addition, these factors have been supplemented with many derived from non-traditional and social science study results.

EXHIBIT P-P:

QUALITY AGE SUCCESS MAPPING

	POSITIVE FACTORS	NEGATIVE FACTORS
Important		
Of some importance		

In the Success Mapping model depicted in EXHIBIT P-P, a format is presented which is similar to the one previously described for scorecard approaches. However, important differences are that in this exhibit, emphases and distinctions are made between "important" and "of some importance" factors and the detail includes many items from the medical/biological realm. The format is depicted in EXHIBIT P-P and the factors listed in EXHIBIT R-R. If a person were to assign, say a value of "3" to each "important" factor and "1" to each "of some importance", a person could judge roughly where they are today relative to his/her chronological age. For example, there are seven positive "important" factors and of these five apply to males and all seven to females. This would be worth potentially 7 X 3, or 21 "years". Also, there are fourteen "of some importance" factors or a possible total of 14 X 1 or 14 "years". The scoring form (EXHIBIT S-S) summarizes this information and provides an application example.

EXHIBIT R-R:

AGING AND SUCCESS STRATEGIES:

POSITIVE FACTORS

IMPORTANT

- Total physical activity
- Blood pressure (normal range)
- Replacement therapy (post-menopausal women; no cancer history) *
- No smoking
- Social relationships: maintain, renew and initiate
- Relaxation/meditative therapies/processes
- Regular breast screening (women) *
- Regular colon screening   *...exhibit continues*

(Exhibit RR continued)

OF SOME IMPORTANCE

- Stamina exercises
- Cholesterol chemistry level management
- Prescribed fruit-vegetable consumption
- Selected vitamin consumption (eg., C, E)
- Selected food consumption (eg., high omega-3 oils)
- Happily married (men) *
- Long-lived grandparents
- Good/satisfying sex life
- Strong, positive life outlook
- Pet owner
- Belief-power of "non-local" spiritual beliefs and practices
- Use of intercessory prayer
- Intuitive knowing
- Belief-power of "non-local" healing intentions

NEGATIVE FACTORS

IMPORTANT

- Heavy cigarette/cigar smoker history; currently heavy smoker
- Extensive exposure to second-hand smoke, environmental smog
- Low HDL cholesterol
- Diabetes out of control
- High body mass index
- Excessive weight gains
- Use of hard drugs

...exhibit continues

(Exhibit RR concluded)

- Personal sense (conviction) of poor health
- Family origin; broken family
- Coronary artery disease
- Parents failed to reach 75 years of age

OF SOME IMPORTANCE

- Infrequent breakfast
- Heavy alcohol consumption
- Driving and drinking
- Significant weight changes
- Fast pulse
- Failure to follow prescription medication instructions
- Regular motorcycle driver
- Failure to use helmet (motorcycle or bike)
- Periodontitis
- Few recommended food groups in diet (nutrition, immune system impact)
- Abusive relationship (women)*
- Failure to have periodic checks; breast (women), colon
- Serious depression
- Poor stress management
- Infrequent use of seat belts
- Regular marijuana use
- Sedentary lifestyle
- Infrequent exercise
- Neither grandparent long-lived
- Lack of social relations, reclusive

* thought to apply primarily to a woman

EXHIBIT S-S

SCORING FOR SUCCESS MAPPING

	POSITIVE		NEGATIVE	
	Important	Of some importance	Important	Of some importance
Men	15	14	33	19
Women	21	13	33	20

Example No. 1:

Mary, age 60, has reviewed the items in EXHIBITS R-R and S-S. She was an early "convert" to non-traditional, "new age" approaches. In addition, she and her husband have greatly reinforced each other's positive health habits, pursuit of daily meditations, and the like. Mary recorded six "important" and eight "of some importance" from the positive factors, and one "important" (parents died before age 75) and one "of some importance" (she doesn't like breakfast and misses some) from the negative factors.

Calculations: Positive points (years): 6 x 3 = 18 plus 8 x 1 = 8 = 26 positive factors   Negative factors: 1 x 3 = 3 plus 1 x 1 = 1 = 4 negative factors

Net: 22 positive factors (26 – 4 = 22)

Her quality of life and longevity expectations from Exhibit 5-5:

Actual age   Success Mapping, Quality of Life, Longevity
60   60 – 22 = 38

Inference: At this point in time, Mary has a quality of life and longevity expectation equivalent to that of about a 40 year old woman.

Note in EXHIBIT S-S that the Mary application example suggests a woman who has been making a major effort (with assists from her husband) to feel good and stay well. If a success mapping approximation were made for her, it might indicate a body of a 40-year old woman and also an excellent outlook for longevity. Note these "numbers" simply provide guides or approximations. These examples should not be taken as an attempt to be precise because the methodology we have followed has been simply to estimate possibilities and gain a general sense of how the person "Mary" is doing. Also, the factor details presented in EXHIBIT R-R provide some specific and tangible bases for fulfilling a person's self-interests in health management while providing an agenda of factors with which to discuss with medical professionals.

Physical and Biological Age; A Note

By "physical age" we are referring to the skeletal structure, strength and functional performance of the individual. A typical physical age situation would be the ability to lift particular weights, raise arms level with the shoulders (and with some restricting force) or climb a flight of stairs without getting out of breath. General experience ("wisdom") would inform one that "physical age" would be linked to one's biological processes reflecting blood flow, clarity of sacs in one's lungs, etc. Thus, they are not exactly the same but clearly are related.

PART IV

❦

Passages: Your Passport to the Future

Chapter IV – 1:

❦

Trip Planning

INTRODUCTION

Some of the happiest moments for many have been collecting trip descriptions and articles about "cool" places to go. Just thinking about some of these trips as destinations often proved exciting and provided a basis for long telephone conversations with friends, dinner conversations, calls to travel agents or searching the Web. Second adulthood and the promise of a relatively joyful experience can be compelling and capture the attention of senior Baby Boomers and older groups (the World War II generation) alike. Hopefully, PARTS I-III have convinced the reader to think of aging as something *much aside* from physical deterioration, sending oldsters out to pasture, rest and entertainment (for those able to afford it) or an exclusive focus on self indulgence. Underlying the discussion of PARTS I-III and explicit in IV is a different type of life and maturity seen but little in past years, yet one becoming more familiar daily and, likely commonplace tomorrow. Job, occupation and career which dominated the outlook and values of the youth culture and society generally in the past are being increasingly supplanted from Second Adulthood lifestyles and values. Terrible life-threatening diseases which dominated the medical scene's top four or five killers in past years are being displaced by disorders and diseases more characteristic of the new "age wave". The person's whole-hearted and beneficial participation in the new Second Adulthood rests squarely in the hands of the person and is a *challenge in individual change.*

This chapter has several purposes. One is to briefly review major Book themes but now in the context of the "Second Adulthood". Second is the need to describe a simple but tested and highly effective model which an individual can use to plan out and individualize a personal change strategy. This model is called "AIMS".[1] It is described in detail in the next section. In addition, some of the most recent findings from aging research and applications are introduced to motivate individual actions and dispel myths arising from the "pop" literature or commonly held societal assumptions.

MIND-BODY HEALTH MYTHS: THE OLD AGING PARADIGM

EXHIBIT IV – 1 A-A

MIND-BODY HEALTH MYTHS: THE OLD AGING PARADIGM

1. A sense that we are always to blame for our own health problems.
2. If you make up your mind to do it, you can stick to an exercise, eating, diet, etc., regime.
3. When we go to a physician to discuss general health problems it reflects a lack of our own self-discipline; we are taking up their valuable time.
4. Seeing a doctor periodically will "keep me safe".
5. My genetic make-up and thus my biology is my destiny.
6. Weight gain is strictly a matter of the "net" of the calories we eat minus the calories we consume.[2]
7. Will power can typically overcome food cravings.

Sources: Heller, Heller & Vagnini (1999); Heller & Heller (1998); and Chopra (1993)[3].

For years the trajectory of aging was often taken to be largely outside of the hands of the individual. Doctors played a central role in health matters and were the "centerpiece" for a therapeutic model of wellness (see the "Old Aging Paradigm", EXHIBIT IV – 1 A-A). People periodically visited their doctor "if they were smart" and somehow this instilled a sense of confidence and good feelings in the individual. Excessive weight meant either a "glandular problem" or the person was eating too much. If it was the latter, it was obviously a lack of will power problem. The person simply wasn't watching what and how much he/she was eating.

Give them a copy of the "food pyramid" for healthy eating, a standard copy of sample dietary menus, and then it was up to the person. Naturally, most responsible physicians checked out the usual vital signs to assure individual safety in dieting, an exercise program, or the like. But then the long-standing assumptions regarding individual health matters and physician roles started to fall apart under the "pelting" of health and related breakthrough medical research, and the collective experiences of hundreds of medical practitioners and individuals.

Breakthrough findings related to the role of carbohydrates in health and health maintenance were typical of the myth shattering findings.[4] Setting aside some of the more technical aspects, these studies helped to clarify the crucial role played by carbohydrates in maintaining the body's hormonal balance. This work helped to uncover mechanisms linking insulin and glycogen. Individual energy, desire for food (for "eating") and thus even the ability to take off and keep off weight, all started to take on more predictable patterns. Hormonal changes, high stress, lack of activity (exercise), dietary fat and food additives, were among the factors that could throw off the delicate biological balance affecting insulin. After effects involved, for example, cravings for food, weight gain (or loss), clotibility of blood, blood pressure and a person's sense of vitality and well being and being in control.[5] These studies revealed that an individual's ability to take off weight and keep it off might often be outside of the individual's control since one's biological make-up and consumption patterns worked against individual resolve or "will power".

Other insights derived from these breakthrough findings suggested that individuals would have to take on much greater responsibility in their own health destiny. Having greater understanding of how these biological processes worked could increase their efficacy in connection with physicians and their control over their health circumstances.

THE NEW AGING PARADIGM

The old model of aging is being radically changed (#1, EXHIBIT IV-1 B-B). The old model emphasized and reinforced the idea of aging as progressive decay and decline. The person played mostly a passive role as his/her life was played out largely on the basis of gene orchestration. However, a new awareness of aging is emerging. People moving into their sixties and seventies, for example, more commonly experience a sense of vigor and health typical of those in their forties and fifties. This is especially true when individuals are motivated and prepared to take on an active role in their health management/lifestyle practices.

EXHIBIT IV – 1 B-B

THE NEW AGING PARADIGM

1. The old model of aging is being radically changed.
2. When people stop "growing", they accelerate the aging process. They become "old".
3. Mind and body, the psychology of being and human biology, are largely inseparable.
4. Individual awareness of self and intentionality regarding lifestyle and health-related processes play central aging roles.
5. A person's experiencing of time affects their state of mind, outlook and sense of well being.
6. Regularly reviewing and renewing one's intention to live an active and meaningful life and then taking appropriate actions can dramatically affect both mental and physical health.
7. Although chronological age is increasing steadily, quality living requires thoughtful health and financial management.
8. Learn to walk the "middle path" between all of life's experiences; seek a balanced and flexible state of mind; embrace complexity and seeming contradictions, and seek to be fully present in the "now".[6]

Sources: Chopra 1993; Heller, Heller & Vagnini 1999; Restak 1997; Gordon 1996; Benson 1996; Weil 1995; Dossey 1993.[7]

When people stop "growing", they accelerate the aging process. They become "old" (#2). Active people typically live longer and with an improved quality of life. New knowledge, insights, skills and ways of viewing the world help to keep body and mind vital. Individual *awareness* of these possibilities, sensitivity to the *impact* they can make in their lives, and *motivation* to build new *skills* and acquire new insights, nurture the growth process.

Mind and body, the psychology of being and human biology, are largely inseparable (#3). The myriad of human cells contain their own form of intelligence; these are frequently programmed through the person's mental processes, habits and lifestyle choices. Thoughts, feelings and senses are all closely linked. Positive thoughts nurture growth, interest and vitality. Negative thoughts projected from one's social and work contacts, or negative self-talk or perceptions, affect the person's functionality and his/her quality and experiencing of life.

Individual awareness of self and intentionality regarding lifestyle and health-related processes play central aging roles (#4). Basic bodily processes respond to the person's outlooks, expectations and state of mind, their awareness. Tardily, medical practitioners and health specialists are just now beginning to use mind-body power for healing. If the person wants to change their body, they must first change their awareness.[8] The body's biochemical processes are importantly affected by awareness characteristics.

A person's experiencing of time affects his/her state of mind, outlook and sense of well being (#5). Individual thought processes tend to constantly shift between past, current and future events and circumstances. A person starts to think about one thing and other thoughts intrude. Periodically, daily, people need to experience quiet as "mind chatter" decreases. Concentrating and focusing on the now, then eventually emptying the mind of all thoughts, meditation provides a powerful means for changing the time reference framework and gaining health and lifestyle benefits. The biological age of long-term *meditators* is significantly less than the chronological age, perhaps by five to ten years.[9]

Regularly reviewing and renewing one's intention to live an active and meaningful life and then take appropriate actions, can dramatically affect both mental and physical health (#6). The simple act of intending to change is an important start for a self-change process. But intentionality must be followed by an action process as new ideas or approaches are launched. People need benchmarks to establish points of departure and realistic goals. Intentionality can eventually lead to individual payoffs in strength, agility, motor abilities, mental dexterity, and the like, but only through persistence and periodic checks. It also follows that the sooner one puts intentionality to work on their behalf, the greater the long-term benefits in quality of life and longevity.

Chronological age is increasing steadily but the concommitant of quality living involves thoughtful health and financial management (#7). The steady advances in longevity and the increased likelihood of decreased retirement benefits from either government or corporate programs has intensified the need for sound financial planning by the individual. Since adequate financial support is a direct product of a time frame, savings and investment activities, launch time is of the essence. It only stands to reason that the best-intentioned health and quality of life planning will run head-on into the reality of the person's financial situation.

TRIP PLANNING IN PERSPECTIVE

Two major themes have dominated "trip planning". One has been the need to dispell common, long-held beliefs that may seriously impede individual health-related change initiatives. The second message of this chapter has been one of outlining and describing a *new paradigm of aging* which for many is likely to represent relatively novel ideas. It is clear that the "age wave" moving through our society has intensified interest in and "new" knowledge regarding aging along with a good quality of life.

Chapter IV – 2:

A Framework for Personal Change

A "GAME PLAN" FOR PERSONAL CHANGE

If an individual is going to undertake a significant change in lifestyle or health-related processes, the guidelines need to be comparatively simple or straightforward, adaptable to a wide variety of situations, and provide a reasonable expectation of valued payoffs or rewards. The "AIMS" model meets these criteria.

Years of research and practical experience in dealing with individual change[1] have provided a simple but powerful model to help guide individual change thinking and approaches.

The "AIMS" model fits many different life situations, personalities, ages and individual needs. "AIMS" is a pneumonic which stands for awareness (A), impact or intention (I), motivation (M) and skills (S). The change will typically involve mind, body or spirit. The change framework is shown in EXHIBIT IV – 2 CC. The following section provides a description of the change format and some examples of its applications.

The Change Framework

Mind, Body or Spirit may serve as a focus for individual change. As established earlier, any of the three elements M, B or S provides an initial basis of change interest or intentions. Eventually, all three should be addressed comprehensively in order to gain the full benefits of synergy and reinforcement among the three factors. EXHIBIT IV-2C-C also suggests that individual interests may be awakened, for example, in a very general way as one becomes aware ("A") of new possibilities to improve one's life, or because of changes which have impacted one's personal life ("I").

EXHIBIT IV – 2 C-C

THE "AIMS" FRAMEWORK
FOR INDIVIDUAL CHANGE

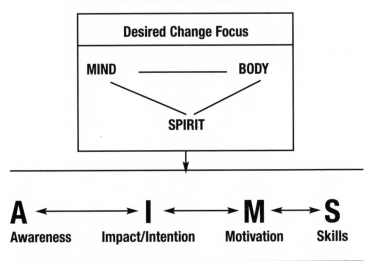

The Change Framework: "AIMS"

The four elements function in an interdependent way. No change is possible until all of the elements have been engaged or energized. Naturally, most real life situations typically defy neat packaging. Thus, highlighting these four elements assists in calling attention to change phases which differ in importance but at times subtle ways. Consider the following simplified example. Helen's friends have often mentioned meditation to her as a wonderful way to relax, get centered and allow things to settle in place. Thus, she has not only become "Aware" of meditation but realizes that there are many times in her typical work day or week when a little meditation could be helpful; she can see the possible relationship or "Impact" on her life. She decides to visit her local library and see what they have on the subject. She is pleasantly surprised to find that there are at least a dozen relatively recent books on the subject of meditation. After reading an elementary treatment of the subject, she compares notes with a friend. The fact that her friend is familiar with some of the meditative techniques makes it relatively easy for her to learn some of the basic approaches ("Skills") and to try these out on herself ("Motivation"). As she became more familiar with meditative techniques, she seeks out more material on the subject and learns that meditation is also highly useful for the creative process. She tries it out on some work-related problems and "bingo"; it really works! She now intends (intentionality) to make meditation a regular part of her daily routines in order to cope with stress, advance her interests at work and simply, to make each day more enjoyable. In this case, Helen has assumed a desired change focus which is at least initially concerned with mental (Mind) processes.

Now we can take Helen's New Paradigm Thinking another step forward. She comes to realize through further reading, personal experience and a class that meditation is likely to have some highly beneficial effects on various biological (Body) processes. Slowed pulse rate, more energy from deeper breathing, and some positive effects on blood pressure are just a few of the benefits which she realizes. (Note how Mind and Body effects start to work together). Eventually, too, new possibilities become accessible for Helen in the spiritual (Spirit) realm as she starts to "see" things going on around her that she never noticed before. She starts to sense a divine or greater presence.

Expanding the Impact of the "AIMS" Model

Having moved through Helen's application situation, let us examine the "models" elements in more detail to suggest the many ways that people become involved with change matters, and are encouraged (motivated) to pursue actions affecting their quality of life.

Awareness (A). The following represents a typical group of situations or incidents so that individuals become more conscious of something which potentially may affect them. Many are self-explanatory.

- Classes, readings, television
- Discussions with friends
- Physical or biological "signals", for example, regularly being out of breath when climbing stairs
- A long look in the mirror, clothes that are not fitting well
- Advice from your doctor after a periodic examination

Impact (I). Here the key point is that the individual can connect up something they have become Aware of with their own situation. "This applies to me." Often these are obvious, but as the New Paradigm developments make clear, often the person doesn't make the connection for lack of knowledge, experience or perhaps a personal model. Take for example, the matter of muscle tone and strength. An older person who has led a largely sedentary life loses muscle tone. Climbing stairs or lifting packages of a certain weight are no longer possible. This individual may require a lot of convincing and exposure to work done in this area that indeed they may be capable of doing a number of these things. From this increased awareness of possibilities, he/she may also develop an intentionality to try out some selected muscle strengthening exercises.

Motivation (M). Numerous factors enter into an individual's decision (motivation) to make changes in his/her lifestyle or health-related activities. In general, all will share the following elements:

1. A belief that the task or procedure is possible (feasible) for them.
2. Knowing how to change, that is, have the skills (S) information or knowhow to undertake change.
3. Having a reasonable expectation that if they do "such and such", *particular results* will follow.
4. The outcomes or particular results will be those which they value (rewarding).

If we take these four motivational elements and apply them to Helen's situation previously described, the following interpretations could be made:

a) Belief; she understood the general thrust of meditative approaches and felt that she was capable of trying out these approaches.
b) Skills to change; she had access to library and class materials plus some coaching from a friend; she was confident of being able to acquire the needed skills.
c) Expectations and results; she had direct knowledge of a person(s) being successful in pursuing meditative practices.
d) Valued outcomes; stress relief and generally feeling better were compelling reasons to pursue meditative approaches.

Common Situations

A person has been overweight for many years and feels (finally) that he needs to take off some weight "for health's sake". Another individual has been told that she "must do something about her blood cholesterol or else run a high risk of ..." . Quite recent medical studies have indicated that either of these situations or both could be related to a form of carbohydrate "addiction"[2]. Thus, long standing weight and high blood cholesterol problems may well require extensive knowledge of this research before any individual change program is undertaken.

A final point needs to be made regarding motivational matters. As brought out in EXHIBIT IV – 2 CC and the ensuing discussion, biological factors for example, may work against an individual's change efforts. Successful change is often far more than simply making up one's mind to change! Consider the following.

Skills (S). The thoughtful conversion of information into knowledge or knowhow is at the heart of acquiring skills. Educational activities, informal and formal, form one of the pillars of skill approaches. A familiar laundry list ranging from books and classes to the World Wide Web is common to these approaches. Another group of potent factors involve people who serve as models of desired behaviors, coaching, counseling, and the like. Also, numerous authoritative health newsletters (eg., University of California, Berkeley, Harvard, Johns-Hopkins and Mayo) are valuable sources of information. Increasing numbers of corporations are introducing pre-retirement health programming and even retirement try-out years before formalizing an individual's departure from the company. It goes without saying that the computer now frequently occupies main stage as a source of information and thereby to build individual knowledge. Finally, increasing numbers of periodicals are publishing all manner of self-administered health-related guides. Many provide an excellent, initial source of "what to look for" and importantly, to start people thinking in greater depth about health-related matters.

THE "AIMS" FOR CHANGE FRAMEWORK: A CONCLUDING NOTE

Much evidence with both successful and unsuccessful individual change efforts has highlighted the need for a systematic framework by which individuals can think through and plan (potentially) a personal change program. The "AIMS" model is one which has proven helpful in numerous instances because it is comparatively simple, adaptable to many situations, and permits focusing on various valued accomplishments. For the "uninitiated", that is, those for whom longevity and healthy lifestyle programming is relatively novel, the question of "where to start?" is answered in a comparatively simple way. Namely, the person breaks into the endless circle of possibilities by tackling initially mind, body or spirit. Naturally, if an imperative exists for a particular undertaking, it assumes first priority. Mind-Body-Spirit all work together. In the end, it is likely that all will be addressed though this may well entail a major (but rewarding) undertaking covering a significant part of a person's lifetime.

PART V

So, What's Next?

Chapter V – 1

Introduction to the "5 R's", Lifestyle and Financial Security Planning

INTRODUCTION TO LIFESTYLE AND
FINANCIAL SECURITY PLANNING

"Retiring Retirement" has served as a theme for an era in which the conclusion of full-time work or long-term employment with a particular employer has become simply another life benchmark. More generally, an era is emerging in which age 65 is becoming less meaningful in terms of lifestyle and longevity. Successful adaptation of health care advances and thoughtful financial planning are all required for quality living and longevity in a newly emerging "Second Adulthood". This is particularly true since "retirement" is no longer being viewed solely as a time of leisure nor of brief duration. Most people will be able to begin a whole new chapter in their life if they choose and for a fast-growing number of Baby Boomers it may turn out to be several "chapters".

It is also clear however, that the Baby Boomers (1946-1965) and the in-between generation and World War II ("G. I.") group, say those born from 1920-1945, are confronted with quite different issues. Both cohorts are huge. The World War II and in-between group is numbered at perhaps 30 to 40 million and the Baby Boomers at over 70 million. Today and for years to come some 9000 Boomers per day will be crossing the 55 years of age marker. "Boomers" grew up in the "New Age" health and lifestyle revolution yet many have meager savings and still need to demonstrate a willingness to adopt various financial and healthful lifestyle practices.[1] "World War II-ers" (the "G.I. Generation") as a group, command considerable financial resources but the differences among group members are great. Some one-third are at the poverty level. Women as a group are significantly worse off than men. All have to confront major personal challenges in adapting to social, cultural and health-related changes during their later years. Although these generational groups have access to the health and lifestyle innovations described in Parts I – IV, exposure and usage differ greatly. Most of the health and lifestyle "innovations" took place when the G.I. Generation was well into their 50's, whereas the Baby Boomers had "innovation exposure" for much of their adult lives. Individual strategies will differ widely because of the great disparity in financial, health, age and other personal circumstances. Part V targets some of these major group differences and also provides a separate section focused on women's financial and health care matters. Discussions are carried out along widely practical lines which can then be "trimmed" to individual circumstances.

SOME BASICS

Even when Mind, Body and Spirit are working together effectively on behalf of the individual, the promise of the "Second Adulthood" may be only a distant possibility unless the finances are either in place or a realistic *plan* exists to bring these about. An underlying issue in this introductory section concerns the very nature of "planning". All planning is linked to the future. All plans and derived strategies will have some level of uncertainty. A *reasonable* level of financial security depends on the person's existing wealth and/or that which can be reasonably planned and *counted* on in the future to match *anticipated expenditures*. The care with which these calculations and processes are carried out and repeated periodically is critical. Seriously entering into the important planning process is a major step forward. For example, survey after survey indicates that *women are less likely to have undertaken sound financial planning than men* yet are likely to outlive men by some six years on the average. Also they often cope with the added costs of a poorer state of health relative to men. It is never too soon to do financial planning but it may be too late relative to one's *preferred lifestyle*. Also, it is hardly ever too late to move into a healthier lifestyle! Flexibility and compromise will often be necessary. This chapter has the purpose of providing a relatively unique planning framework for undertaking financial and "5 R" analyses. By the "5 R's" we mean rest, recreation, refuel, retool and/or re-career.

Topics related to the "financials" have become so specialized that expert status is virtually required to pursue these in depth. The amount of available information from books, the Internet and consultants is overwhelming. Thus we have opted to pursue an approach that emphasizes the "5 R's" and some financial essentials related to these. A short bibliography containing useful financial/career lifestyle information is also provided at the conclusion of this chapter. Also, the Internet provides increasingly useful sources.

Many ideas associated with the "5 R Model" were developed in the last chapter but a few points need clarification now since they directly affect the "financials." Rest and Recreation (R & R) as concepts, emerged out of the World War II days and were meant to suggest a badly needed but temporary respite from the high tension and stress of combat life. In the current context, taking a break from a lifetime of working is often a necessary first step in the passage to the "Second Adulthood". Some may well opt to stay in this lifestyle pattern indefinitely. Thus the financial needs would likely center on travel, continuing education, visits with grandchildren and the like. However, many choose to "Refuel" energies and interests that could well involve a year or two. Then "Retooling" might well involve starting to learn new skills, new patterns of work-play-learn, etc., to see if these newer possibilities add value or meaning into one's life. Finally, "Re-career" could signal a whole new lifestyle and work pattern drawing on the insights and wisdom gained from all of the other past phases. The schematic which follows, Exhibit V – 1 AA, summarizes these approaches

Consciously or otherwise, all of us have learned to live with uncertainty in our lives. Who lives and who dies; who gets cancer and when; getting married (?); having children (?); and promised payouts from health or pension plans, are part of the fabric of life. These various life cycle events occur in "real life" and contain varying degrees of uncertainty or predictability. Individual circumstances differ so greatly so that these analyses must be built around individual circumstances. Sensible plans and strategies can be put together even though varying degrees of uncertainty must be accommodated.

PLANNING FLEXIBILITY

The fast-growing sophistication of planning processes provides some useful principles and models to facilitate "5 R" processes. Thoughtful individual plans are likely to contain elements drawn from these various planning models.

EXHIBIT V – 1 AA

FINANCIAL PLANNING AND THE "5 R" MODEL: NEEDS ANALYSIS APPROACH

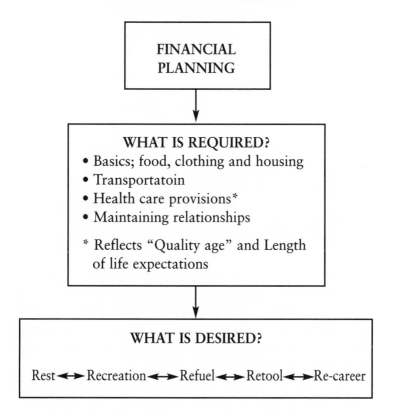

FINANCIAL
PLANNING

WHAT IS REQUIRED?
- Basics; food, clothing and housing
- Transportatoin
- Health care provisions*
- Maintaining relationships

* Reflects "Quality age" and Length of life expectations

WHAT IS DESIRED?

Rest ◄►Recreation◄►Refuel◄►Retool◄►Re-career

Tracking models. The essence of this idea is that emerging trends are carefully noted, analyzed and then become the basis for reshaping strategies as circumstances continue to change. For example, a good general investment strategy for people in their mid-40's and mid-50's may be a portfolio of quality bond holdings of 25%

and 50% respectively. However, changing regional, market or corporate circumstances often dictate important short or longer run changes in investment strategies. Another example would involve changes in one's health circumstances. Undertaking and demonstrating to oneself a sustainable and positive change in lifestyle circumstances (e.g., giving up smoking, dealing with obesity, or exposure to environmental pollution) may lead to a realistic reduction in the re-estimate of health cost contingency needs. In short, the thinking derived from extensive experience with tracking models is to monitor the environment of one's circumstances for significant and changing circumstances and then to start to factor these into financial planning.

Contingency Models. Highly volatile and/or fast changing circumstances may rule out attempting to anticipate and regularly adapt to change. It may be more reasonable to define the best and worst scenarios and situations likely to occur and then to attempt to estimate the likelihood of these eventualities. Prudent individuals may then balance the risk by, for example, investing more of their financial portfolio in relatively solid (low-risk) securities or investment instruments and the rest in more speculative issues.

A PLANNING FRAMEWORK:
IMPORTANT IDEAS WITH SIMPLE PACKAGING

The "5 R" framework described in the previous section establishes the basis for setting down ideas and calculations at one's own planning table (PC or whatever) and running through some key ideas and calculations. A description used for the overall process diagrammed in Exhibit V – I – AA is termed "needs analysis". Bedrock is "what's required?". "Food, clothing and housing", "maintaining relationships", "transportation" and "health care provisions" form the core of these. A creative picture of "what's desired?" spells out some of the key and individually focused elements of the "5 R" picture. These comprise the individual's "desired lifestyle". Desired lifestyle translates into numerous activities and processes, all of which carry a "price tag". Common ideas include a few weeks in Arizona or South Florida during the winter, continuing education, volunteerism, attendance at Elderhostel programs ("most anytime, anywhere, any subject and at moderate prices"), periodic visits out of town with the grandchildren, and club memberships. However, most anybody's life/lifestyle planning approaches can be benefited by awareness of the experience and views of the seasoned experts whose knowledge cuts across the many fields contributing to these approaches. Prominent among these specialists are gerontologists and career and financial planners. We have distilled out three categories and 13 guide points from the voluminous work of literally dozens of experts in these areas.

SOME INVESTMENT AND LIFESTYLE GUIDELINES

The 13 points that follow have passed the basic litmus test of usefulness. All are specific enough to provide some actionable approaches by the individual yet general enough to fit widely differing circumstances.

THE "5 R" PLANNING PERSPECTIVE

1) At most every life stage, a person has choices to make and options to pursue which afford a considerable degree of individual control.

2) *"5 R" planning is longer term planning.* Modifications of one's basic investment strategy are avoided unless irreconcilable changes in circumstances have taken place.

3) *Lifestyle stages* suggest naturally occurring events in the *rhythm of life.* Moving beyond full-time work, becoming an "empty nester", "second adulthood" marriage, divorce or death, relocation, and even volunteerism, are examples of events the timing of which coincide with an individual's life cycle stages.

4) *Preserving one's options* while trying out newer "Second Adulthood" directions maximizes subsequent personal value and enjoyment. Thus, for example, the opportunity provided by a company for "retirement tryout," or renting a home or apartment initially, rather than purchasing and making a major lifestyle commitment.

"Savings" Philosophy

5) *Better sooner than later.* Getting into the savings habit as early as possible increases the likelihood of successfully accumulating and having available adequate assets when these are needed. Also, this approach expands possible options which can be pursued.

6) *Money's time value* is increased only when it is used productively and not simply accumulated. Money needs to work on behalf of the person. The individual has a personal obligation to optimize financial returns commensurate with safety and the person's allowable risk situation.

7) Wisely invested money *compounds* in value. The value of these funds at any given time in the future is (much) more than a simple multiple of the amount saved per unit of time.

8) Savings/investment *intentions* represent a veritable minefield of *lost opportunities*. Most surveys reveal that the actual realized savings are either non-existent or often far less than past intentions.

9) It is *never too late* to launch a savings/investment plan but it may be too late to achieve the lifestyle desired at an earlier life stage. Those plans may have to be modified or drastically changed. Don't delay; take action NOW.

Thinking Through Investment Strategies

10) *While employed, invest as much as possible* in a recognized and sponsored savings plan (e.g., 401-K's). These plans are often contributed to by the employer and can help to shield investment earnings and funds from current taxes.

11) *All future plans* are embedded in *uncertainty*. The further out in time the targeted objective, the greater the uncertainty. Developing contingency plans and working with investment experts on

factoring uncertainty into a particular plan is desirable and necessary.

12) One person's judgment regarding the future and strategies may not be as good as another. Working with highly qualified people who have a demonstrated "track record" is prudent. This is an area well worth researching prior to making an investment commitment.

13) Esoteric and/or high-risk investment schemes are to be avoided. Unless the individual can absorb potential losses without throwing off their basic investment strategy, these approaches are to be disregarded.

A format for lifestyle/life investment/savings planning follows in Exhibit V-1-BB. It is in a *"needs analysis"* format. This particular needs analysis helps to identify possible sources of future income and to make comparisons with the costs of a) meeting basic life needs, and b) more creative "second adulthood" activities suggested by "5 R" analyses.

EXHIBIT V – I BB
GENERAL NEEDS ANALYSIS: LIFESTYLE/LIFE PLANNING

Today's Date: _____ Current "Quality Age" (QA): _____
Life Expectancy (re: QA): _____
Planning Horizons (yrs): _____
Important Assumptions: _____

A) **What is Required? Describe**	**Estimated Costs**		
	One time	**Annual**	**Total***
Food, clothing & housing			

* Add notes as needed

...exhibit continues

Exhibit V-I BB *(continued)*

Transportation

Health care

Relationships

B) What is Desired?* Describe   Estimated Costs
One time   Annual Total

Rest

Recreation

Refuel

Re-tool

Re-career

* (add notes as needed)

C) Anticipated Income   Estimated Net Income
Annual   Total
1. Continuing work? (part-time, full-time,
   spousal income, etc.)
2. "Retirement" plans
   Social Security
   Corporate/School
   Other: _____
3. Liquidity
   a) Accumulated savings

   _____
   _____

   b) Value of investments

   _____
   _____

...exhibit continues

Exhibit V-I BB *(concluded)*

   c) Property

      _____

      _____

   d) Other

      _____

      _____

4. Inherited wealth

      _____

D) **Summary:**
   1. What is required?   Overall cost $_____
      Avg. cost per yr. $_____
   2. What is desired?   Overall cost $_____
      Avg. cost per yr. $_____
   3. Anticipated income?   Available per year $_____
      Special timing? Access?

When the "General Needs Analysis" is completed, several similar and useful sets of calculations can also be carried out. Perhaps the most useful approach to these is to consider the *"General Needs Analysis" as only one of a set of calculations which can be carried out with varying assumptions regarding income, health and longevity factors.* For example, health care provisions can be raised or lowered; longevity can be further extended or reduced; or different "inherited wealth" assumptions can be used. As various assumptions and calculations are tried out in the General Needs Analysis form, the "answers" start to define an area of cost-income possibilities. In short, this area defines the most likely range of situations the person will face in future years. This approach is highly useful because it starts to factor in many different life circumstances which cannot be accounted for by a single set of calculations. Uncertainty is thus factored into individual planning in a practical way and various contingencies can be anticipated.

Chapter V – 2

The Financials, Health Care and
Women's Issues

THE FINANCIALS: A SHORT "CRASH COURSE"

Financial planning for mid-life, retirement and beyond has finally caught on. Companies, schools and other institutions provide "retirement previews" and financial planning services. The Internet and the shelves of popular bookstores such as Border's and Barnes & Noble provide dozens of books related to this topic. This has become an area of expertly trained professionals, a field unto itself. Thus, we will confine our discussion to a few basic and key features and related health issues.

Some of the substance of this particular chapter is borne by simple tables and assumptions corresponding to common but diverse situations. Additionally, the tables are arranged from relatively simple to more complex situations. Since each person's situations differ widely, an end-of-chapter summary is provided to simplify referral.

WOMEN, AGING AND FINANCIAL REALITIES

Many women's groups have long recognized that aging is a major women's issue. Now, health research groups and general demographic studies confirm what is already widely known by women. The Henry J. Kaiser Family Foundation is one of the leaders in investigating and highlighting women's related issues. Highlights of some of their reports including their Medicare Beneficiary Survey (1996)[1] are as follows.

- At birth, women's life expectancy is some six years longer than that of a man's.
- Women account for about 55% of Medicare payments from age 65 to 74; some 60% from age 75 to 84, about 70% from the 85+ category.

- The nursing home population and home health care services are skewed towards women; some two-thirds are females.
- For those who are poor, the number of females exceeds that of men by much. For individuals with less than $10,000 per year of income, women are the dubious leaders of this group. In the age category 65 to 84, the statistics indicate that there are some 30% women versus 15% men. After age 85 and above, women in this low-income category are some 55% compared with 27% for men.
- For those suffering poverty (about $7700 per year income or less in 1996), women again come out on "top". Nearly 7 in 10 of Medicare beneficiaries living below the poverty line are women.
- Women tend to initiate the savings habit at a later point in their lives than men.[2] Thus, women tend to live longer and are more economically insecure. The women's issues become even more compelling since they confront more chronic and poor health conditions and consequently become more dependent on safety-net programs.[3] However, if we were to end the discussion with these rather dismal notes, we would be doing a disservice to the female reader.

The "5 R" lifestyle/life framework described in this book encompasses numerous means by which the individual (woman) can start to beneficially take charge of their (her) life. The conception of "Quality Age" which encompasses good health practices (e.g. nutrition, exercise, diet, non-smoking, meditation and maintaining relationships), includes many approaches largely independent of income. Further, female access to good health support and practices in the future also seems a likely consequence of the mounting debate to expand elderly aid. These would include prescription drug coverage under Medicare.

Women are also urged to pursue other practical options focused on taking charge of their lives. These include the following:[4]

- Secure much good financial planning information.
- Elevate personal financial security to high-priority status.
- Control spending, especially since control of expenses and debt are significant women's issues.
- Put together a savings and investment strategy and start it.
- Make women's financial security "necessary income and expense" items.
- Start on the plan as soon as possible.

HEALTH CARE: COSTS AND THE "R" GENERATION

Most older "Boomers" and seniors don't want to think about taking on the costs of acute health care. The "war stories" abound of people's life savings going down the seemingly bottomless health care drain and in a comparatively short time. The (seemingly) quick passage of time is no illusion; about 50 percent of health care expenditures are made in the last six months of life! Major illnesses such as Alzheimer's are among the 50 percent. Other illnesses can drain funds over a period of years.[5]

Most people lack comprehensive health care coverage

and a disturbing number, perhaps 25 to 30 percent, lack any coverage at all. Thus, if a major illness strikes, the individual (or couple) is forced to turn too often to meager savings which are depleted very quickly. At this point, many are forced to seek Medicare (if eligible) or are forced to seek public assistance, as for example, Medicaid. Even for those eligible for Medicare assistance, there has not been a history of consistent governmental (congressional) support.

There is no quick fix for these kinds of situations, but there are some growing, positive developments due to advances in health care technology and in healthful living and planning techniques.

There is no longer doubt that good nutrition, exercise and thoughtful health habits can reduce the severity and frequency of illness. Thus, the staggering costs often associated with disease and acute health care can be mitigated. Virtually anybody at any time can (start to) get into the improved health mode of living and reap the benefits in a comparatively short time. Realizing these savings has great import too for extending health care coverage and/or reducing relative health care expenditures.

The Home Health Care Saga:
A Bright Light at the End of the Tunnel?

Home health care was and is a good idea.[6] Home health care delivery means that patients receive competent medical care in the home where medical needs do not involve hospital technology and organization. There is an amazing array of medical situations readily lending themselves to the home health care mode. Usually, a competent registered nurse (RN) is the "point person" for service delivery. Through periodic visits, the nurse or assistant responds to patient needs and often trains somebody in the household to share these responsibilities (under supervision). Thus, medical/health delivery costs are held down. In-hospital costs are reduced and individuals usually recover more rapidly in an atmosphere of family, friends and home. Although national figures indicate a rapid rise in the costs of home health care delivery, a competent balance sheet would show the simultaneous reduction in the costs of hospitals and other health care units. The Budget Act of 1997, however, changed much of this.

The Budget Act of 1997 devastated the availability of home health care services. Budget reductions forced Medicare to withdraw many support services in home health delivery. In some cases, up to one-third of these services was eliminated. Nationally, some 500 home health care units closed their doors (subsequent to the 1997 actions) and in highly populated states, this amounted to incredibly large numbers. In the State of Illinois for example, some 70 units were put out of business. However, there was a bit of hope in this otherwise bleak picture.

As of Fall 2000/Spring 2001, a "perspective health care system" is supposed to be rolled out. *If* everything moves on schedule (!), more reimbursements will be authorized on the basis of individual patient needs. If indeed this system becomes functional, it means that competent health care services will then be accessible to millions of additional people.

Additional reinforcement and extension of home

health care services appear imminent due to the remarkable advances in technology-based information/communications systems. The hopeful speculations of the 1990's seem very likely to materialize in the areas of both health care diagnostics and delivery. Local and regional computer-based systems will facilitate vital-sign readings from remote locations. Family members and others will be trained over health/medical networks by competent health professionals.

New "Prescription" for Health Care Coverage?

As yet it is not exactly a stampede but major insurance health care companies are starting to move towards some type of coverage for "alternative" health care therapies.[7] Many are finally conceding that which has been a fact of life for better than 10 years. There has been a strong and growing trend to the use of alternative medical treatments with some four out of ten Americans using these therapies. In the past, most had to fully absorb these cost expenditures. But even this is now starting to change. For example, one large health plan (offered by a health insurance company), is said to be offering member discounts (partial coverage) of up to 20 to 25 percent for some 25 different procedures including Chinese herbal medicines, massage, meditation and yoga. Access to practitioners of these approaches will also be facilitated. The health plan referenced here is already on record for the coverage of chiropractic care (which is now mandated by the state) and acupuncture, which is physician-prescribed.

PLANNING FLEXIBILITY: NEW TECHNIQUES

The fast-growing sophistication of planning processes provides some useful principles and models to facilitate "5 R" processes. Thoughtful individual plans are likely to contain elements drawn from these various planning models.

Tracking Models: the essence of this idea is that emerging trends are carefully noted, analyzed and thus become the basis for reshaping strategies as circumstances continue to change. For example, a good general investment strategy for people in their mid-40's and mid-50's might be a portfolio of quality bond holdings of 25% and 50% respectively. However, changing regional market or corporate circumstances often dictate important short or longer run changes in investment strategies. Another example would involve changes in one's health circumstances. Undertaking and demonstrating to oneself a sustainable and positive change in lifestyle circumstances (e.g., reducing weight or giving up smoking, dealing with obesity or reducing exposure to environmental pollution) may dictate a realistic reduction in health cost contingency needs. In short, the monitoring and assessment of one's circumstances for significant changes becomes the basis for factoring these into one's financial planning.

Contingency Models. Highly volatile and/or fast changing circumstances may rule out attempting to track and regularly adapt to change. It may be more reasonable to define best and worst case scenarios (situations likely to occur) and then to attempt to estimate the likelihood of these eventualities. Prudent individuals may then balance the risk by, for example, investing more of their financial portfolio in relatively solid (low-risk) securities or investment instruments and the rest in more speculative undertakings.

DRAWING THE ELEMENTS TOGETHER

The latter half of life, corresponding roughly to the years subsequent to age 45, is a remarkable period of individual change, but it also has great financial implications. Aside from a fortunate few who already (apparently?) have secured their financial future, future *financial security* for most people still awaits the initiating actions of thoughtful financial planning. In the transitional period from perhaps 45 to 64 years of age, declarations of future intentions - - work or retire or re-career or rest and recreation - - are tempered by the unfolding realities of each person's life. The latter includes "Quality Age" (reflecting lifestyle and state of health), psychological state, family/marriage issues and financial matters. Superimposing the template of aging demographics on top of financial matters suggests several quite different financial scenarios. At one extreme, some 70 million Baby Boomers are starting to flood across the age 55 marker. This amounts to some 9,000 to 10,000 per day who are in fact seeing their previous lifestyle thoughts and perhaps plans played out against the realities of their emerging life pattern.

At the other end of the age spectrum, the World War II generation (born before 1927) are actively living out past dreams and current realities. Clearly, savings, financial planning and spending patterns for these disparate groups are very different. For those at the younger end of the age range, even the initiation of short(er) range savings and investment programs can bring about significant financial results! The simplified portrayal of various financial investment strategies (EXHIBITS V-2 AA through 2 EE) brings out the different value of alternate strategies with varying returns (and risks) as well as missed opportunities from starting late.

Major wild cards in the financial planning picture are the likely future direction of health and medical technology (age extensions), costs of acute health care delivery and health benefits coverage. Long term health care policies and "assisted living" arrangements represent some increasingly popular hedges or flexible strategies to deal with some of the uncertainties. See the end-of-chapter notes. Another chapter theme deals with the special financial problems confronting women. Added years of life (versus men), poor health and lower earnings often due to caretaker roles, pose significant challenges in reasonably approaching, let alone achieving, financial security. However, individuals are in a position to significantly affect their future prospects if Book themes are actively incorporated into their lives.

The general needs analysis format presented in this chapter provides a framework for integrating lifestyle/life planning with financial matters. Additionally, if a series of calculations are carried out based on various but realistic assumptions, a planning framework is established which is likely to prove highly valuable. Additionally, as unexpected future events present themselves, these can be incorporated into the financial planning framework.

The value of thoughtful savings and investment planning is often lost in the absence of some concrete numbers and calculations. The following sections provide a short "crash course" on these investment essentials plus some examples. There is no effort here to be exhaustive;

SOME BASIC FINANCIAL REALITIES
EXHIBITS V – 2 AA through 2 EE**
Overview

2 AA)   Late-in-life savers
2 BB)   To reach an end-of-period amount
2 CC)   Savings accumulations – alternate strategies
2 DD)   Results – alternate investment strategies
2 EE)   Popular investment schemes

Key Features
Table No.

V – 2 AA comparison of late-in-life savers with savings ranging
from 10 to 20 years. In addition, alternate annual savings figures are compared.

V – 2 BB Investors are assumed to have determined the appropriate amount desired at the end of a 20-year savings
period. A conservative 6% rate of return is assumed.

V – 2 CC Compares the accumulated savings over a 20-year
period of a $1000 per year savings strategy at a some-
what optimistic rate of return at 10%. For individuals
wanting to check out annual savings schemes for multi-
ples of $1000, these are equal to a simple multiplier of
the indicated value. For example, $3000 per year would
lead to a value of 3 x $39,000, ($117,000) at age 64.
Also, appropriate figures can be determined for a start
at virtually any age (excluding for the moment tax considerations).

V – 2 DD This illustrates some alternate investment strategies for
employed "Baby Boomers" accessible to an employer's
401K plan. Two different savings schemes are compared.

V – 2 EE This table provides several popular investment
approaches involving the 401K, a Simple IRA, a Roth IRA
and a non-deductible IRA. A rather significant number of
assumptions are also included.

** All exhibits and figures only for general illustrative purposes. See a
competent financial advisor for (your) specifics.

EXHIBIT V – 2 AA

**ALTERNATIVE SAVINGS STRATEGIES FOR
LATE-IN-LIFE SAVERS**

Assumed interest rate ("conservative") = 6%

Annual Savings ($)	Length of Savings (yrs)	End-of-period Accumulation ($)
$1000	10	$15,800
$1000	15	$24,700
$4000	15	$99,000
$1000	20	$36,000
$4000	20	$144,000
$5000	0	$194,000
$10,000	20	$389,000

Note: all numbers are rounded: no tax considerations included

...more

EXHIBIT V – 2 BB

**ALTERNATIVE PAYOUT STRATEGIES;
LUMP SUM VALUE AT END OF PERIOD**

Assumed rate of return (conservative) = 6% (net before taxes)

Savings period = 20 years

Desired Value at End-of-period	Annual Savings (schedule) Required
$100,000	$2700
$200,000	$5150
$300,000	$7700

...more

EXHIBIT V – 2 CC

THE POWER OF THE SAVINGS HABIT

Assumptions: Age 44
"Retirement" age 64 (withdrawals to start)
Annual investment $1000
Account earning 10%
Annual taxes on earned interest

Age in Years	Elapsed Time in Years	Approximate Value*
44		start
49	5	$6000
54	10	$14,000
59	5	$24,700
64	20	$39,000

* Net after taxes on the interest savings

...more

EXHIBIT V – 2 DD

SOME ALTERNATE "BOOMER" INVESTMENT STRATEGIES

Objective: $IMM+ at age(s) 65-67

	Current Age: 40	50
Household Income	$84,000	$84,000
$ Retirement Objective / year (% of current income before taxes)	80% ($67,200)	80% ($67,200)
Savings Strategy (401K) (% of salary, every year)	10% ($8,400)	15% ($12,600)
"Retirement" Instrument (employed person)	401K	401K
Employer's Matching Funds (assumed)	50%	50%
Assumed Earnings on Funds Saved *	10%	10%

* Slightly below 60 year average market rate of return.
  Based on calculations in Ellis (1997) and Simmons and
  MacBean (2000)[8]

EXHIBIT V – 2 EE

ALTERNATE RETIREMENT SCHEMES: RETIREMENT SECURITY OR HOW LONG DOES THE MONEY LAST?

Assumptions:

- Age 44
- Retirement age 64 (withdrawals start)
- Annual investment $1000
- Account earnings 8%
- Annual withdrawal (starting at age 64) $5000
- For employer contributory plan (401K), employer matches $.50 per dollar saved. It is also assumed that the individual is in the 33% tax bracket (state and federal)
- Annual savings (from taxes) are reinvested at 5%

Plans	Approximate total savings at age 64	Approx. age at which savings/ income would be exhausted
401K	$91,000	95
Simple IRA	$86,000	97
Roth IRA	$45,000	79
Non-deductible IRA	$45,000	75

Based on "The Great Savings Derby".[9]

** This and all Exhibits V-2 AA through 2 EE for illustrative purposes only See a competent financial advisor for (your) specifics.

plenty of reference materials exist regarding these subjects. This section also includes some notes regarding future directions for health care costs which may prove useful regarding "provisions for health care".

Tentative Conclusions: The Financials**

The five exhibits presented in this section have had the purpose of illustrating important themes and "principles" described earlier. The most basic point is to get into the savings habit early. The value of future savings or investments at a particular point in time depends directly on the time provided for the money to increase in value. In "5 R" planning, individuals were urged to lean towards good quality and relatively low-risk approaches. The cost of obtaining expert advice usually turns out to be a bargain in terms of future monetary returns and lessening the mental trauma of non-planning, "taking a chance" or speculation with scarce funds. Although it is never too late to start thoughtful financial planning, one's preferred lifestyle directly affects the saver's time provisions.

** Exhibit V-2 AA through 2 EE for general illustrative purposes. See a competent financial advisor for (your) specifics.

SELECTED BIBLIOGRAPHY: THE FINANCIALS

Bernstein, Bill (1999). *The Intelligent Asset Allocator: Portfolio Theory for the Small Investor*. Coos Bay, OR: Bill Bernstein private downloadable book available through www.EfficientFrontier.com

Bianchi, Eugene C. (1994). *Elder Wisdoms: Crafting Your Own Elderhood*. NY: Crossroad.

Business Week (July 19, 1999). "Building the Best Retirement Plans". Special issue written by the editorial staff of *Business Week* magazine and covering a variety of retirement, health care delivery and cost matters. NY: McGraw-Hill.

Ellis, Junius (1997). *Your Top Investing Moves for Retirement*. NY: Money Books, Time, Inc.

"Focus on Health" (1999). Chicago Matters, WBEZ Chicago Public Radio, Chicago, IL.

Focus on Long-term Care (1995). A special publication developed by the Emerald Publications Organization, 12395 World Trade Drive, San Diego, CA, 92128-3743.

Fortune (August 17, 1998). "The Richest Day of Your Life" and related articles by the Fortune editorial staff: 110-124.

Oliver, Gene (1998). *Life and the Art of Change*. Costa Mesa, CA: Life Change Press.

Shilling, Dana (1999). *Financial Planning for the Older Client*. Cincinnati, OH: National Underwriter.

Simmons, Henry C. and MacBean, E. Craig (2000). *Thriving After 55*. Richmond, VA: Prime Dynamics.

Miscellaneous Sources:

Publications of AARP, especially dealing with economic security/work issues, the "AARP Women's Initiative" and Working Age.

Employee Benefits Research Institute.

Scudder Market Research including studies of Baby Boomers.

Merrill Lynch, Annual Retirement and Financial Planning Survey.

National Association of Personal Financial Advisors.

Women's Institute for a Secure Retirement.

Older Women's League.

National Council of Women's Organizations.

Chapter V – 3

Spirituality

INTRODUCTION

What is the rationale for a chapter on spirituality in a book focused on "Retiring Retirement"? It is a good question for which the answers start to open up themes which will be given attention in this and the remaining chapters. First, as people start approaching mid-life transitions, the sense of aging is inescapable, but so are questions like the "meaning of life", "maintaining the quality of living" and "how to cope with aging?" "Spirituality" understandings and strategies may be able to answer in part the "how" or "why" questions as well as supply some specific strategies to accomplish these. Second, the onset of a "new age" of breakthroughs in holistic thinking about and experiencing life envisions spirituality as inexorably connected to mind and body in (hopefully) a balanced, unified whole. Undertakings which benefit body or mind will also nourish the spirit. Correspondingly, activities which strengthen the spirit may also benefit "mind" or "body". Thus, having a healthy active life often brings untold rewards to an individual's quality of life and this may also result in enriching the lives of others, too.

SPIRITUALITY POWER

A characteristic of the New American Spirituality is the reshaping, even reinvention of traditional religious ideas and precepts to meet individual needs.[1] Although these reformative efforts appear to be frequently within (or to draw from) particular religious frameworks, this customizing of beliefs and behaviors clearly departs widely from traditional practices. Furthermore, individualization and re-framing of moral, religious and living precepts takes place over many years and culminates at a later point in the individual's life. Active re-framing seems to culminate around the onset of the "Second Adulthood", say 40 to 50 years of age. Thus, meditative practices, Buddhist wisdom, and Jewish Kabbalah, for example, may be prominent in one person's (new) belief/practice approach. This re-framing of spirituality for the person typically follows years of testing out "ideas" and various contacts with many belief systems and the experiencing of life-defining events (e.g., illness and the death of loved ones, friends or family members). More generally, it often reflects the growth of wisdom (for the person) built on numerous and diverse life experiences. It represents a kind of "democratizing" of the spiritual journey and life with the burden of decision-making placed squarely on the individual.[2]

Features of individual spirituality are linked to "body and mind" to form a holistic belief and behavioral framework customized to individual needs.[3] As spirituality is further shaped and defined by the person, sensitivity and intuitive insights regarding health matters, among others, are likely to grow. A sense of connection and communication with a "wise and compassionate essence" within and without the person energizes these intuitions regarding an ultimate ordering of things and health and well-being.[4] Another frequent occurrence is accepting the unexplained; "this is the way it is supposed to be".

A HOLISTIC PERSPECTIVE

"New Age" and holistic thinking envision quite a different set of formally cherished societal values and the role, functions and goals of the individual. Spirituality is transcendent as suggested in the attached Exhibit V – 3 AA and inseparable from Mind and Body, discussed in Parts I – IV.

Our thoughts are transmitted as electrical impulses through the central nervous system and nerve branches throughout the body. Breathing and food intake and exercise fuel chemical and biological processes which affect all manner of bodily functions including the immune system. These same chemical and biological processes affect mental processes and even the quality of thoughts and perceptual activity. Spirit affects peace of mind and immune functions; it can in part affect stress containment and the person's sense of well being. Thus, basic precepts of this book are that:

- Body and mind are connected
- Body and spirit are connected
- Mind and spirit are connected
- Body, mind and spirit form an interconnected whole

This holistic perspective and societal changes provided a foundation for the emergence of newer societal values.

Newer Societal Values

In the old economy and society we accepted the dominant reign of science and technology. Included were

EXHIBIT V – 3 AA

MIND, BODY AND SPIRIT: A HOLISTIC PERSPECTIVE

Fashioning a Concept of Spirituality for Ourselves:
- Gaining a transcendent vision of oneself and potential.
- Searching for eternal wisdom.
- Seeking to gain truth about existence for self.
- Blending masculine and feminine values.
- Developing compassion and forgiveness.
- Clarifying our own morality, seeking enlightenment and recognizing our mortality.
- Conducting the "quest" for our creative soul.
- Delving into the nature of the universe.
- Discovering our passions, loves; becoming fully alive; and then "going for it"!
- Artfully achieving a sense of divinity, a divine essence, being or notion of God apart from religious form or building on religious notions.
- Accepting life, death, grief and pain as part of the natural order of things, of nature.

For a more detailed discussion of many of these points, see Lesser (1999).[5]

central societal values that expressed the good life which was interpreted in terms of an automobile (or two), a home, making (much) money and even more recently, dexterity in using the computer. A work career was a paramount and central life activity. So also was wealth accumulation towards the day in the future when we would retire. Rites of passage for the end-of-life encompassed and often centered on medical technology and the medical community and institutions.

The national order of values was the accepted order of things and formally established religion, the sole path to bliss.[6] "New Age" thinking has critically examined these assumptions, values and foci.

A newer mission of people is one of a never ending process of self-improvement and a life and lifestyle for which the person needs to assume full responsibility as both "trip planner" and "plan executor". Through mindfulness (awareness and active thinking about our role, relationships and bodily functions) and heartfulness, love and compassion for and in relationships nurtured with experiences and growing wisdom, a new agenda has grown. *The holistically focused, new economy person bravely searches out a newer or more complete understanding of existence for himself/herself.*

The word "bravely" is intended because the quest will unearth notions of living the full life which includes life and death as part of a natural order of things (Exhibit V-3 AA). The focus is on balance as a person discovers within himself/herself beneficial masculine and feminine values, the combination of which can elevate (transcend) ideas of what is good or bad, right or wrong, and ineffective or effective. Self-sacrifice will often be part of a new order of living in which the person both accepts and even desires that the priorities or values of others prevail in situations where his/hers were the only ones that counted in the past. See Lesser[7] for a detailed discussion of these points.

SPIRITUALITY; THE "HEART" OF THE MATTER

The "heart" of individual spirituality rests on a foundation of intentions and the soul's journey of explanation and accomplishment of these.[8] With aging and hopefully the growth of wisdom, individual intentions frequently turn towards more noble purposes. The intention grows to experience the presence of the divine or infallible being (God) which we "know" is there. This is because of such things as logic-defying events, unexplained occurrences and the growth of a personal sense of confidence that "this is the way it is".

The soul's journey of exploration and actions to accomplish intentions require clear goals and the desire to live a more spiritual life. This might well include: "feeling" God's presence; seeking aid or support from the divine one (e.g., the strength to break unhealthful habits); experiencing a richer life with meaning and purpose in living; a noble and clear vision or aspirations; and the motivation or will to accomplish these.[9] All qualities possessed by humans: love, creativity, "emotional intelligence", and truth among others; are almost boundless.

With the widespread (older) societal focus on goals, careers, lifestyle and "fulfillment", it is quite easy to associate individual intentions with earthly activities and the strong values linked to these by society. These notwithstanding, the intentions (intentionality) discussed here have to do with those linked to the soul's journey and nurturing our spiritual lives. As actions are taken which seemingly support these spiritual aspirations, they began to reinforce the resolve to undertake more of these types of actions in the future; and make them an integral part of the person's life.

Earlier, a reference was made to the intertwining of both "good" and "bad" experiences. It is perhaps a paradox that achieving "good" judgment depends on having made bad judgments. Thus, a rich background of experiences must include past bad judgments and the learnings derived from these. In the past, "bad" experiences were most often accompanied by negative emotions, guilt, hopelessness, rage, fear and envy among others. The old drivers of money or prestige, however, didn't seem to work anymore. Also, wishes of bad things for others such as job failure, breaking up of a love affair, envy because of expensive cars or clothes or exotic trips, need to be rooted out and critically examined as to how these detract from our own life purposes. The source of some of these negative feelings may be buried far back in our childhood and require our coming to grips with early family or life experiences. Professional assistance may be required to unearth these really deep-seated feelings and experiences.

A Closer Look at "Noble" Intentions

Mature people too often have accumulated much baggage which clutters up their lives and their ability to experience "worthy" visions. "Bad" experiences are tangled up with "good" experiences and lessons to be learned are remote or unclear. And then, of course, there is even a more basic question here which is "who decides what is worthy or noble?" Let's look first at the basics. In the first half of life, "First Adulthood", parents and religious institutions ("external" to the person) were typically "in charge" of defining worthy or noble activities, often with a distinct moral and religious overtone. In the "Second Adulthood", the person takes on (internally) the mantle of defining for himself/herself what is worthy or noble. Individuals have had the benefit of many years of life experiences which provided a testing ground for tempering the moral and religious guides which tended to dominate the first half of their lives.

Noble intentions also "spring" from individuals and institutions which serve as models of higher aspirations, worthy deeds and modes of accomplishing these. Lifetime learning experiences which open up new avenues of learning from history or inspirational stories may seem to be almost miraculous. These include: miraculous recoveries; people who outlived length-of-life predictions; the 76-year old woman who daily lifts 80-pound weights; and the 86-year old man who regularly runs a 20km race. These are typical of "miracles" which surround all of our lives. We simply need to look at what is going on around us. "Do you get it?"

Some new learnings take place simply by doing or experiencing new actions or behaviors. Deeds of loving kindness bring enormous personal gratification and represent an example of how one builds a repertoire of noble thoughts and actions. Also, new learnings often imply that old feelings and the emotions attached to these must be discarded; the person must be prepared and willing to change!

Spirituality, Meditation and Coping with Stress

A useful and excellent example of holistic thinking and applying ideas discussed in this chapter relates to coping with stress. Everybody's life contains varying degrees of stress at any given time. However, being overly stressed may also be a serious challenge to individual healthfulness and welfare when it gets out-of-bounds and for an extended time period. The growing intensity of work experiences, lengthening of the work day and work week, depersonalization of relationships and growing computer dependency, extensions in length-of-life and the fast growing pace of disruptive social and environmental changes, have elevated stress levels and have made it a widespread societal problem. It challenges individual well being, both mentally and physically. Meditation increasingly is being exploited by individuals to quiet the mind (and nervous system) and provide a basis for sound stress-coping strategies.

It has been well substantiated that meditation can induce a "relaxation response" which nurtures individual insights, creativity and more healthful living styles.[10] To the extent that meditation gets us in touch with our body and mind (e.g., "What is going on with me?", "How is this affecting me?"), individual insights are enlarged and surrounding events take on new (less threatening) meanings. We start to "notice" the true wonders of nature and how these in turn can help get things back in perspective and elevate the spirit at the same time. "What we see depends on where we stand". Also, as stated in the Talmud: "We do not see things as they are. We see things as we are". Thus, meditation's nourishment of individual mindfulness can simultaneously provide: a) a new lens for viewing stress sources and events, b) calm nerves, and c) shift focus towards a greater sense of connection to nature, the universe and a divine essence. The latter is the core of spirituality.

FROM AGING TO "SAGING"

Perhaps one of the most profound expressions of spirituality is the individual's transformation from "aging to sage-ing". Rabbi Zalman Schachter-Shalomi's (1995)[11] philosophical pronouncements (he uses "age-ing" to "sage-ing"®) are the genesis of this exciting concept. It represents a new psycho-spiritual model of individual development. In the Rabbi's view, the re-framing of aging represents an opportunity for unparalleled inner growth. Individual consciousness (mindfulness) is extended which in part offsets a (possible) reduction in physical skills or social relationships due to aging. This culminating stage of spiritual development witnesses "old age" as an opportunity and period of wisdom-extension. It is truly a significant breakthrough in spirituality, mindfulness and exemplary lifestyle thinking.[12]

Rabbi Zalman mused about the possibilities of transforming the "extra" years of life due to medical/technological advances. This could well be a period of unparalleled growth in wisdom and its exploitation to better oneself emotionally and spiritually and the lot of others as well. Reaching the late 50's in age, apprehensions increase regarding growing "old".

The Rabbi initiated his own "vision quest"; he sought a vision of his own life purposes in this ancient rite-of-passage tradition. Meditation and discussions with people of many faiths were part of his "quest". The culmination of this exploratory journey was a major legacy for his and subsequent generations. His quest and progressive refinement of thinking centered on several key steps and inquiry areas:

1. Regrets about lack of accomplishment in case of imminent death.
2. Meditating on one's loved ones and prayers for their welfare.
3. Writing notes to loved ones expressing sentiments which had often gone unsaid.

Converting his "vision quest" into a new life for himself became the culminating act. Tangible guidelines were provided by a wholly new set of personal and professional priorities. He then started to enact these within his personal and professional life.[13] One of the tangible expressions of his accomplishments was marked by the founding of the Spiritual Eldering Institute (SEI). The spiritual and psychological tools gained by the thousands of people enrolled in SEI workshops subsequently proved to be a gateway to rethinking aging assumptions in the lives of participants and many others, too. For many it became a "transformative experience".

The transformative experience meant becoming an "elder" in our modern culture and time. The acceleration of the "new" age wave and the onset of the aging society were forcing a rethinking of the "youth culture" idea. It also involved a critical examination of aging assumptions regarding such attributes as wisdom, self-knowledge and even physical and mental capabilities. Thus;

40 was becoming the *new* 30!

50 was becoming the *new* 40!

60 was becoming the *new* 50!

70 was becoming the *new* 60!

It started to become clear that in no small part, a self-confirming aging model had been operative in the culture and society with negative images and expectations strongly reinforced. New values, assumptions and beliefs were being shaped that would result in a radically changed picture of growing older, aging and old!

Schachter-Shalomi's "New" Model of Late-life Development and Spiritual Growth

The heart of the Rabbi's vision was a process whereby "older people could become (or were) spiritually radiant, physically vital and socially responsible".[14] Growing wisdom was both derived from and enacted in a "spiritual eldering" process in order to achieve a successful elderhood.[15] A new notion of an "elder" relevant to our society was emerging. The Live Oak Institute (1977) defined an "elder" as a person still growing and learning and thus creating a viable connection to their future.

The promise of "life, liberty and the pursuit of happiness" was as much of an entitlement for the senior person as for a youth! An "elder" in this view was one who both deserved and received respect because of their thoughtful synthesis of wisdom distilled from their life experiences. The Rabbi's synthesis of personal wisdom truly became a "legacy" for future generations!

A SPIRITUALLY BASED PROCESS FOR SENIORS

In a previous chapter, we referred to a "5 R" process (rest, relaxation, re-tool, etc.) to facilitate the transformative activities of "Second Adulthood". A rich, almost infinite combination of life activities result with each custom fitted to individual situations. However common to all in the "spiritual eldering" perspective were numerous "giving back" undertakings. These encompass but are not limited to: framing a true legacy for one's family; acts of love and empathy in connection with those with whom we are regularly in contact; and various community and environmental service projects. Many individuals might well choose to maintain some level of work activity with former employers or new ones. Also, for any given individual, the lifestyle elements would continue to change as life circumstances changed. However, the key point is that these are now part of a repertoire of activities, perspectives and emotional experiences characterizing a successful elderhood!

RESETTING THE SPIRITUAL CLOCK: MOVING INTO A SUCCESSFUL ELDERHOOD JOURNEY

Moving into, creating, and then embracing a positive elderhood role is easily one of life's most difficult transitions. For most people, the vision quest and its accomplishment is a transformative experience. There is little or nothing in one's past life to serve as a model or guideline. The early educational process provided a highly structured life for some 16 years. Work experiences stretched out for 30 to 40 years with numerous people providing companionship, experience sharing and models of how to do it. Long term employment with a single employer was common. Societal conventions defined major life events involving birth, marriage, raising children, graduation and even rites surrounding death. The personal experiences of a colleague illustrate some of the difficulties encountered in "resetting one's own spiritual clock" to a new lifestyle and eldering life.

A Personal Odyssey; Case Study

It wasn't until "Joe", a colleague, was in his late 50's that his studies of organizational and policy issues increasingly related to ageism and the performance and better utilization of "older" people. His analyses also started to become more of a personal challenge as well. In retrospect, it was remarkable that despite years of dealing with aging matters and working in it as a major research field, he was able to hold these at arm's length and avoided their becoming a personal emotional encounter. As an aside, it turns out that many in their 50's and even 60's have balked at fully confronting their own aging and how this might impact their lives. However, over the next three or four years, all of this changed. He immersed himself in these matters and while still engaged in full-time work at the University's Research Institute. His emotional baptism into the world of aging and defining a route through the transition into "second adulthood" drew on numerous and diverse resources. It may prove useful to list some of these since these are accessible to all.

SOURCES

Books (written)
Books (audio)
Video tapes
Magazines (e.g., New Age, Modern Maturity)
Health newsletters (e.g., from sources such as Johns-Hopkins, Hanrard, and the Mayo Clinic)
Seminars, workshops and classes
The Internet and TV specials
Friends

There are three observations that need to be made regarding this list of items. The first general point is that no single resource or even small number will suffice to push the person through the denial barrier and to undertake the "quest" towards a fertile area of positive thoughts and actions. Most beneficial is that of drawing on multiple resources, having discussions, and then allowing these to play out in one's thoughts over an extended time interval (anywhere from one to three years!).

The second point concerns the item "Friends". Our experience has been that their "knowledge" and experiences must be approached in a highly critical way. As often as not many friends are suffering for lack of good information in their own lives. Although it is true that a friend can serve as an excellent model of desirable aging, this is an exception rather than the rule.

The third general point is that there are many practical differences between a) information or philosophical discussions versus distilled wisdom meant to prepare the person for his/her own mortality, and b) personal processes and techniques defining or describing one's "Second Adulthood" activities. For example, books by Schachter-Shalomi (1995), Chopra (1999), Gallup (2000) and Lesser (1999)[16] are quite helpful in opening up aging issues and starting the mind's incubation on and probing of these matters. Murphy and Hudson (1998), Orloff (2000)[17] and the fast growing literature on exercise, healthful eating and meditation, are examples of highly useful application sources of workable techniques and approaches. Joe started to sort out and make these distinctions.

By the early 60's, this person was well into both planning and doing. Planning included studying the likely direction and costs of health related needs, even if healthful imperatives of nutrition, exercise and personal habits were actively pursued. These included several different assumptions regarding "state of 'future' health". Second, planning also indicated that with reasonable life expectations (out to 85 or 90 years of age), his financial resources would be hard pressed unless he was able to create more wealth as for example, building up a larger pension fund. These financial analyses led to a decision to delay his "retirement" from active university teaching from 65 to 70 years of age. Thus by age 72, he and his wife had pursued the "5 R" framework consciously in their lives for some five to seven years. In retrospect, it appeared that financial assessments made in his early 60's had pretty well proved to be viable some ten years later.

IN PERSPECTIVE

No small part of one's spiritual quest is the recognition that mind, body and spirit are inexorably joined together. Crafting thought patterns, activities and relationships which benefit one of the components has a positive impact on the others as well. The spiritual quest, an increasingly important theme of later life activities, possesses the potential to become a life fulfilling journey for the person and a start in answering the question; "What is life all about?"

Chapter V – 4

A New Path – "Second Adulthood"

MOVING SMOOTHLY ONTO THE NEW SECOND ADULTHOOD TRACK: PASSAGES, STAGES, TRANSITIONS

This "chapter" is a short, bridging one focused on the process of transitioning or passages *common* to *all* individual change activities. Discovering the new passages available to the individual and then planning and making decisions are central to the previous and following discussions.

A central message throughout this book is that the unprecedented improvement in longevity has brought unique quality of life possibilities but also much greater uncertainty and thus unpredictability. While people live longer and may mature earlier physically, they take longer to grow up emotionally.[1] Although many women are starting to develop new belief systems, values and ways of viewing life and their possibilities, many men seem confused regarding the consequences of the new "Age Wave" revolution for their life and work roles, relationships and future possibilities. Old model "game" rules and simple tallies of accomplishments or success, for example, wealth, home, degrees or titles are being replaced rapidly (but still unbeknownst to many men!) by larger, more complex sets of roles, activities and goals. These include: mentor, father, husband, caretaker, one who is "giving back", environmental steward, (spiritual) elder, and prudent, community-wise person. The possibilities have grown rapidly for creative mental stretching and taking on wholly new personal and societal roles. But this will only happen if men are prepared to shed the old (armour) coat of long-standing habits, expectations, life assumptions and traditional markers of advancement or accomplishment. In short, to think through and then "print out" a wholly new travel map for their lives.

SURVIVORS

An unfortunate but realistic conclusion from survival statistics is that one marriage partner will outlive the other, often by a number of years. Further, the stats suggest at least six years favoring the female. However, in a more general sense, the impact of premature or early deaths really starts to become apparent in the late-40's into the mid-50's. The death of parents, relatives, and long-time friends increasingly become part of the living experience. Indeed, dying is a natural part of life. Thus, the Second Adulthood years will likely include some number of years, few we hope, without a loved partner. Although as indicated, the survivor is likely to be the female member, both men and women have to be prepared for this eventuality. Individuals must be able to *re*-group or *re*organize their lives. People may be plunged suddenly into highly unfamiliar roles including that of financial planner or caretaker.

A Major Male Challenge

At this point, another bit of realism enters the picture. And this is that most women find an easier transition to living as a single than men. From almost their earliest age, women have developed interpersonal communications skills and a circle of intimates. Moving into support groups, whether focused on relieving the felt-loss of a partner, or even a post-trauma group (e.g., cancer), is an easier, near-"natural" move for women generally. Too often, when men are dealing with the aftermath of death, they withdraw from contacts and formats involving interactions with others. An alternate and common strategy is to continue working. Understandably, the latter approach soaks up the need for personal thinking or planning time. Many of these responses to death are contrary to the Second Adulthood strategies described in this book. "5 R" approaches apply even more so under these circumstances. Major religions such as Judaism counsel a mourning period for the deceased but also the sanctity of life for the living and the need to move on in one's life despite the loss of a loved one.

Century 2000 Relationships and Partnering After Adversity

Many individuals, whether men or women, feel the need for intimacy. Typically this calls for (re)establishing relationships and/or some partnering arrangement, which can only be approximated by spending some or perhaps much time together. Having "someone who cares about us" and backs this up with thoughtful, even loving acts of concern. Many have worked out various types of contemporary living arrangements *aside* from marriage. (Note: this discussion simply reports on what has apparently worked well on behalf of the people involved. No moral judgment is being rendered here.) Some couples have chosen to (simply) live together because of numerous economic complications. Some argue the likely loss or decrease of Social Security income if they re-marry. Others have concerns regarding the legal complications of inheritance. *Regardless of the rationale advanced, maintaining or re-establishing close, even intimate relationships is a paramount need.* Many will continue to search out that arrangement which best fits their circumstances.

THE CHALLENGE OF (AND RESISTANCE TO) INDIVIDUAL CHANGE

Reluctance to make lifestyle changes is the central personal challenge of a fulfilling "Second Adulthood". Do the following scenarios and comments seem familiar?

2 years ago: "Dorothy, how about signing up for one of those classes at the "Oasis center?"

1-1/2 years ago: "Dorothy, do you remember those Oasis classes I told you about?"

1 year ago: "Those Oasis classes are great...have you signed up for any?"

3 months ago: "Dorothy, I am going to register for the next term at Oasis...got some great classes...how about it?"

Last week: "Well, didn't I tell you that you would like it?" "My calendar's loaded – – but I still have time to go over to the club for a workout."

Although these scenarios are likely familiar, the plain facts are that people are changing, even those who appeared to be a "lost cause" in the past. However, in all fairness, it must be said that lifestyle changes in general are difficult, but even more so with the deeply etched experiences of the older "Second Adulthood".

Continuity, Aging and Adaptation to Change

Conventional wisdom informs us that most people unconsciously adjust themselves to changing circumstances. Adaptive changes at any given time are usually modest ones and not especially noticeable. Thus individuals tend to age successfully when they are able to maintain balance in life, continuity, by preserving a general pattern of thoughts, behaviors, relationships and lifestyle.[2] Discontinuities occur when the general pattern must be consciously, often significantly altered in order to cope.

Another important continuity perspective is the idea that successful aging may be adversely affected where an individual has vested heavily in job or family roles, for example.[3] Downsizing (loss of a job), death of a family member, even a seemingly lovely event like a son or daughter getting married, can touch off severe individual responses for a parent, if that person has directed much of their life energies to the job or one's family. Clinging to the past when these (large) discontinuities occur can undermine mental or physical health. However, there is another side to this matter of *continuity* which can also prove to be disruptive.

At the extreme, as a person ages, they may yearn for *stability*; "I want off this merry-go-round of life". On the one hand, this is unrealistic relative to the "normal" changes in one's physical and mental structure and environmental circumstances. On the other hand, many developments are taking place in one's environment which could prove highly beneficial if the person is prepared to acknowledge these and perhaps even exploit them for their purposes. For example, personal computers (PC's) have brought world events, health advances and all manners of information to the individual's threshold (see Chapter V-8). The fast expanding availability of adult learning programs including Elderhostel and the various Institutes for Learning in Retirement, promise new mind expanding experiences. Thus, the person needs to keep an open mind (and time) to pursue these newer learning avenues and break out of the seeming comfort of "continuity'-like activities and behaviors which draw too heavily on the past.

THE NEW AGE FOCUS AND
THE NEW "SECOND ADULTHOOD"

Millions of people including many Second Adulthooders are constructing the foundation and building blocks of a post capitalist, people-oriented society.[4] Determined individuals are pioneering new work, service and leisure time modes. They are: deepening spiritual practices; undertaking health self-management responsibilities in partnership with medical people; pursuing non-traditional health practices including holistic health, and supporting spiritually responsible businesses. Also, they are swelling the volunteer ranks of schools, hospitals and all kinds of service groups (local to international); and serving as (guardian) stewards for our natural (and national) resources. Some even view themselves as members of a global community comprised of people and organizations creating a just, compassionate and sustainable future. They include: blue and white-collar workers and executives; farmers; the poor and the wealthy; union members; teachers; housewives, widows and widowers, and business owners. They increasingly support groups like Common Ground and Common Cause and publications like *The Nature Conservatory*, and numerous quality health newsletters as *Yes! Positive Futures Network*. Chapters V-5 through V-8 outline some of the substantive conflict and activities of the *new* "Second Adulthood" track. These are truly exciting times!

Chapter V – 5

Planning for a "Second Adulthood"

A "SECOND ADULTHOOD":
A BIT OF PLANNING OR JUST LET IT HAPPEN?

The idea of a "Second Adulthood" has already been referenced in some of the previous chapters. This chapter provides some of the background for emergence of the Second Adulthood concept, fleshes out some of the highly useful ideas associated with it, and then frames these within a broader planning approach for quality living and longevity.

In her national best seller, *New Passages*, Gail Sheehy[1] mapped out a new concept of adult life across time. A new Second Adulthood in mid-life was emerging. Older descriptions and points of adulthood demarcation were being permanently altered. Thus, the old paradigm spanning the ages 21 to 65 was no longer particularly meaningful. The new Second Adulthood paradigm (see EXHIBIT V-5 FF) for those who embraced it, spanned perhaps the ages of 45 to 85 years. It embraced the ideas of deeper meaning, relationships and opportunities to express human potential. Its validity is being increasingly documented by an unprecedented extension of life expectancy and functional abilities. However, there is *nothing automatic about gaining the promise.* Planning related matters must eventually be addressed.

However, the lack of attention to quality living and longevity is now starting to change, and rather quickly! The ideas and approaches described in this Book are becoming part of a "critical mass" accelerating change to New Second Adulthood thinking and activities. Books such as Real Age (Roizen, 1999) and Sheehy's books *New Passages* (1995) and *Understanding Men's Passages* (1998)[2] eventually became national best sellers and

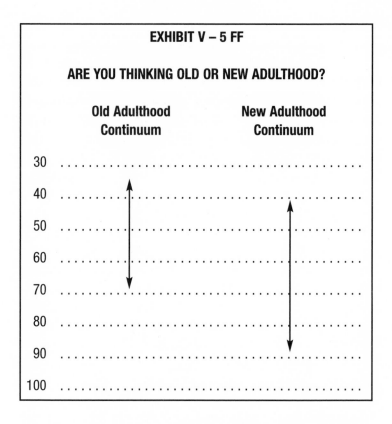

EXHIBIT V – 5 FF

ARE YOU THINKING OLD OR NEW ADULTHOOD?

| Old Adulthood Continuum | New Adulthood Continuum |

reference guides for personal planning and change. Better than one out of two adults are now experiencing some type of continuing learning experience annually. And, even some of the most traditional type newspapers and periodicals are now regularly featuring articles or sections regarding aging, healthful living and educational matters, among others. Nobody knows for sure what the future will bring but even a few contingency plans ("What if...?") and contacts with some of the knowledgeable people in this field can start to improve the person's chances for fruitful future living.

Defining Activities

Various defining activities have become generally associated with different stages of the "Second Adulthood". These dovetail naturally into traditional work and life pursuits. Collectively, they represent a call to serious critical thinking *and* action for individuals entering these stages of personal development. Great detail or high specificity has been consciously avoided here, recognizing the need to tailor plans to individual circumstances. Generalized approaches also are much more in keeping with the nature of life itself.

Exhibit V-5 GG possesses two characteristic features; one is "Quality Age" and the other, life passage-defining activities through the new Second Adulthood. The reader may recall that "Quality Age" was an attempt to represent the person's real age by taking into account his/her health, physical condition, psychological outlook, dietary habits and even family history among other factors (see previous Chapter). People are urged to discuss and sketch out the results of their analyses (the life cycles/transitions notes) at various convenient points. A simple diary or notebook and dates help to anchor personal experiences. It is important to identify and record things which did and did not work and learnings from these and intended next steps.

The New "Second Adulthood" Paradigm

Life extension and more healthful living have provided individual access to activities, relationships and experiences which may prove to be unique in the life of a given person. Expanding wisdom, gaining new skills and

---

EXHIBIT V – 5 GG

CHARACTERISTIC LIFE CYCLE STAGES AND PASSAGES INTO AND THROUGH THE NEW SECOND ADULTHOOD

"Quality Age"	Characteristic or Defining Activities/Processes (see Note)
30	Career preparation and advancement
	Career advancement
40	
	Initial reflections on health and aging matters
	Start "Life Cycles/Transitions Notes"
50	
	Active participation in wellness/aging discussions
60	Upgrading Life Cycles/Transitions Notes
	"Retirement"/Re-careering tryouts
70	Living elderhood; creating and transmitting a legacy for future generations
80	Transmitting your legacy to future generations
	Life completion and closure rituals
90	

Note: "Quality Age is *not* the same as chronological age (see Chapter). "Quality Age" takes into account such factors as psychological outlook, lifestyle and nutritional activities. It can differ greatly from chronological age.

experiences, "stewardship" actions relative to our natural resources and mentoring younger people represent but a few of the opportunities being actively pursued by growing numbers of Second Adulthood people. Enjoying the fruits of a lifetime of full-time work or family caring has much to be said for it but need not be the exclusive focus of Second Adulthood planning and living patterns. These and related points are summarized in Exhibit V-5 HH.

The optimism of people entering wholeheartedly into Second Adulthood and successful aging activities is well expressed by the White Crane Wellness Center in Chicago. The essence is as follows:

> I am a good person
> I am a healthy person
> I am building a strong body
> Good people come into my life
> I choose to be happy!

Planning Issues and Approaches

Many people are passive, scared or even hostile when it comes to concentrating on their future. Even self-serving financial decisions with demonstrable payoffs in the future are frequently delayed. Eventually, these may be forgotten altogether. Just consider the experience of people and their attempts to shake off health-threatening habits such as overeating (obesity), smoking and drinking. True, a small cadre of self-actualized people may have anticipated what has become known as a (new) "Second Adulthood". These Second Adulthood needs include location, living arrangements, medical, housing and continuing education

---

EXHIBIT V – 5 HH

**THE PROMISE OF THE NEW ADULTHOOD PARADIGM:
A SPIRITUAL/RELIGIOUS PERSPECTIVE**

- *Life extension with new(er)* fulfillment and contribution opportunities, in our lifetime.
- New opportunities to coalesce/synthesize one's experiences and reflections, deepen wisdom, and benefit others (individuals, community and society) and nature/environment.
- New mentoring and "giving back" opportunities, e.g., "spiritual eldering"[®], community projects and charities.
- Uncovering and discovering new meanings for aging and old age.
- Compiling personal/family histories; lending new meanings to one's roots and providing a legacy for future generations.
- Transcending personal motivation and gratification. Examples include: a custodial role with planetary implications; maintaining a vibrant planet joined by a web of organic relationships and furthering relationships which are loving and respectful.
- Enjoying, at least in part, the fruits of a lifetime of work and family care--not just a reward in heaven or the world to come.

For a rich discussion on many of these points, see Schachter-Shalomi.[3]

---

arrangements. But for the most part, a new Second Adulthood continuum stretching out 15, 20 or even 25 years beyond the old adulthood model has not been fully acknowledged by Baby Boomers and less so by those born before 1946 (see EXHBIT V-5 FF). Most people just seemed to be letting events unfold, i.e., "letting it happen".

Books and articles dealing with future life matters, though often interesting, appeared especially timely—but for someone else! It seems to be a lot easier to let events play out or to avoid thinking about something "over which I have no control anyhow". On the other hand, "planning" too presents numerous challenges. One of these is dealing thoughtfully with uncertainty.

A final general point concerning "planning' is the uncertainty attached to the process. At any given time, the person does the best job possible based on available information and their own (common sense and) experience. Over time, as circumstances continue to change, the individual must return to the plan to assure its continuing relevance or to make needed adjustments.

SECOND ADULTHOOD: SOME PLANNING STRATEGIES

Although Second Adulthood can take on many different and specific forms, the key is to recognize one's current situation for what it is. It largely determines the scope and detail of the activity. For example:

a) For Nancy, a 45 year old department manager, Second Adulthood planning came down to financial analyses and next moves in a career planning framework. A critical part of this included longer term financial planning.

b) At age 55, Jim was only recently hired after almost two years of unemployment. Health-wise and financially, Jim had to aggressively play catch-up while trying to piece together a positive and realistic picture for enacting his Second Adulthood.

c) Maureen and Harold, both in their late 60's, had been married for almost 30 years. Both were "retired". Only recently had they started to talk about the possibilities of living many more years. Once a week trips to the health club, golf, cards, lunches and friends occupied had most of their time. No conversation had ever included talking about a future in which one partner outlived the other.

d) Selma, 74 years of age, had been a widow for almost 10 years. Fortunately, she had been adequately provided for (financially). She played tennis three or four times a week. Additionally, she played cards, talked to friends, and travel occupied most of her time. Two years ago, one of her friends had "dragged' her to a health care presentation by a local hospital representative. From that point on she was "hooked'. The following month she registered for some courses at the local Oasis Learning Center which included one on nutrition and the other on travel. Selma came to realize that she could significantly improve her diet and exercise program to gain the fullest benefits for quality of life and longevity.

Spiritualizing Aging; A Modest Game Plan to Get Started

For those who have not as yet had the opportunity to meditate or think more deeply about their future life possibilities, a few practical ideas may prove useful. These ideas are summarized in Exhibit V-5 II and discussed briefly below.

EXHIBIT V – 5 II

**GETTING DOWN TO THE PERSON'S CREATIVE CORE OF IDEAS:
THE START OF A SPRITUALIZED GAME PLAN**

1. *Schedule regular personal reflection,* note-taking and "noodling" time.
2. Attend or create group formats where aging and related matters are likely to be discussed. *Unearth your ideas and assumptions (and myths!) about aging!*
3. *Seek out and identify individuals as models* of exemplary behavior or those *whose instruction/training are likely to provide useful philosophies, guidelines and techniques.*
4. Maintain a journal or *record ideas, contacts, and your own emotions, feelings and reflections.*
5. Provide plenty of *incubation time* to allow ideas to ferment; *nurture those which seem to be promising but do not make "early" final choices as to what to pursue.*
6. Define markers of progress; g*ain closure* on analyses *to reinforce your efforts. Reward yourself as benchmarks of progress are achieved.*

Even when people have "retired" there never seems to be enough time to do what needs to be done. Hours slip into days, weeks and months. Thus, the quicker the person gets through the chatter and things which are always coming up, the better the creative incubation time and the better the result. Getting down to the person's creative core, "spiritualizing" the aging experience, is the start of a highly productive process. Realistically it will take months or years to unfold. Exhibit V-5 II summarizes some of the

197

practical tips for getting in the mood and producing a useful result.

It often turns out that the individual has to (mentally) calendar meditative or reflective time. Much material exists on meditation and the creative process.[4] Formal meditation can take place in the home, a secluded spot or even at work. Jotting down ideas (Points Nos. 1, 4 and 5) are especially valuable and helps to ensure mental encoding and a basis upon which future thinking can be built.

Many formats exist where the ambiance or very presence of particular people both stimulate thought and provide specific, useful ideas. Corporate retirement planning sessions, professional meetings, lifelong learning sessions and videotapes are among the many possibilities. However, common sense care must be exercised in discussions with acquaintances or friends. Many have grown used to viewing the person in a particular way and much of the person's potential may have been missed, even by friends of long standing.

This potentially valuable information source of talking through ideas with individuals can be quite dysfunctional if the people in the discussion network are sour on, or reject out of hand, planning discussions dealing with one's future.

Models of valued behaviors or lifestyles (Point No. 3) is an underused but highly productive source of ideas and practical activities. When somebody says "I feel better doing 'such and such'" or when useful information is provided, it is time to take careful note. Also, getting particular, mature Baby Boomers or older adults to share "how they did it", can prove very valuable.

A last point is the need to define personal progress markers for the individual's search process (Point No. 6). A loose framework of activities, events and times helps to keep the process moving forward. By "times" is meant general time targets as for example, "by Christmas", or "by the end of my vacation", or "by the end of the trip", or "by early spring".

Chapter V – 6

Sorting Things Out and Making Decisions

THREE MAJOR "SECOND ADULTHOOD" DECISIONS

Understandably, many people are preoccupied with taking care of current, let alone future, financial matters. Society's near worship of the dollar in terms of conspicuous consumption, prestige and universal use in all kinds of transactions, have elevated money's role to one of almost unique importance. What is often forgotten, however, is the often-complex relation of income and financial resources to numerous personal preferences and decisions. There is no question that financial matters must receive high priority and arguably be the first point of attack in one's future planning. This said, it is a logical *starting point;* but only that. Many experience a flush of confidence and even a sense of gaining closure after reviewing their financial matters and even drawing up a will with their lawyer. It is our contention and experience that the individual must then start to factor in at least two other areas of thought to (even) round out the person's initial planning foundation (see Exhibit V-6 JJ).

One's intended "lifestyle" and "location" preferences have a major bearing on the financial picture or vice versa. For example, regarding "lifestyle", philanthropy and even volunteerism may entail added financial needs. Similarly, access to family, friends, support groups or specific types of people (e.g. age) will affect a location decision and thereby a particular cost-of-living structure. One's state of health (a critical part of "Quality Age") and commitment to healthful living, will affect planned-for fund sources including set-asides, or "rainy day" contingency funds.

Many points in Exhibit V-6 JJ are self-evident but several may prove useful to flesh out.

EXHIBIT V – 6 JJ
THREE MAJOR SECOND ADULTHOOD DECISIONS

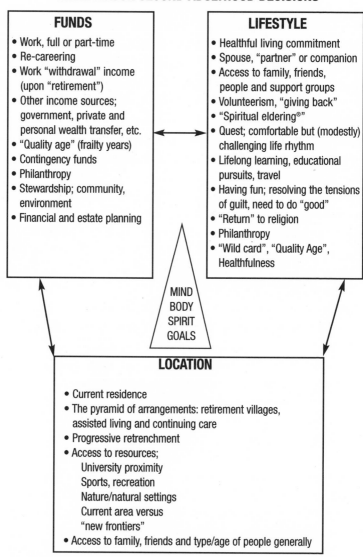

FUNDS

- Work, full or part-time
- Re-careering
- Work "withdrawal" income (upon "retirement")
- Other income sources; government, private and personal wealth transfer, etc.
- "Quality age" (frailty years)
- Contingency funds
- Philanthropy
- Stewardship; community, environment
- Financial and estate planning

LIFESTYLE

- Healthful living commitment
- Spouse, "partner" or companion
- Access to family, friends, people and support groups
- Volunteerism, "giving back"
- "Spiritual eldering®"
- Quest; comfortable but (modestly) challenging life rhythm
- Lifelong learning, educational pursuits, travel
- Having fun; resolving the tensions of guilt, need to do "good"
- "Return" to religion
- Philanthropy
- "Wild card", "Quality Age", Healthfulness

MIND
BODY
SPIRIT
GOALS

LOCATION

- Current residence
- The pyramid of arrangements: retirement villages, assisted living and continuing care
- Progressive retrenchment
- Access to resources;
    University proximity
    Sports, recreation
    Nature/natural settings
    Current area versus
    "new frontiers"
- Access to family, friends and type/age of people generally

Note: For an especially useful discussion, see Simons and MacBean (1999)[1] on these and related points.

FRAILTY YEARS

The health experience of people in late adult years varies tremendously. Where people have adopted healthful living patterns, as suggested by "Quality Age", a period of fast health decline or rapidly rising health care costs tends to be minimized. Naturally, there are no guarantees when it comes to planning for the frailty years or period. We can only go on the general or overall experience. The odds favor those who have adopted healthful lifestyles. If in addition one's ancestry favored healthful, long lives, future possibilities are even more promising.

Since "frailty" planning is relatively unique to the background and experiences of most people, we have summarized some of the particulars for this type of approach (see Exhibit V-6 KK). For ease in planning, points have been organized into two main categories *of Spiritual Eldering® advocated and which was developed by Rabbi Schachter-Shalomi (1995).* The role one plays, for example, in connection with peers, family members or in an intergenerational mode, may well prove to be a defining feature in a person's mature adult years. Sharing wisdom and lending a helping hand are typically highly gratifying experiences. In some communities, especially through the efforts of the Spiritual Eldering Institute (SPI), founded by Rabbi Zalmon-Shalomi Schachter, "Spiritual Eldering®" circles have been established. These help to formalize the process of wisdom and help sharing. SPI provides "training of the trainer" workshops for people assuming leadership responsibilities in community-based, "Spiritual Eldering®" groups.

Location. This has become a far more complex decision area because of the numerous options now

---

EXHIBIT V – 6 KK
"FRAILTY" PLANNING FOR DAILY LIVING

A) The Ability to Function in a
Residential (limited) Environment

Bathing, ability to keep oneself clean.

Continence; bowel and bladder
control.

Dressing; including the affixing of a
prosthesis.

Eating; ability to feed oneself.

Food preparation; in house or outside.

Toileting; ability to use toilet and
maintain personal hygiene, including
cleanliness and personal appearance.

Transferring; mobility in and out of a
bed or chair.

Medication/Health; ability to take
prescribed medications; seek help as
needed.

Housework; maintain clean conditions
(or supervision of these).

B) The Ability to Function in the
(broader) Community

Shopping.

Accounting; timely payment of bills,
management of savings and transfer
of funds.

Transportation; drive or arrange for
transportation; mobility to use public
transport.

Communication; establish/maintain
links; stay abreast of developments.

Volunteerism

Maintaining relationships; meeting at
remote sites.

* Usually associated with "being old" or one's declining years.

For a useful discussion of some of these points see Simmons and MacBean
(2000) and the Mayo Clinic (1998) Health Letters.[2]

Note; Medicare was designed primarily for acute care and neither it nor
Medicaid are likely to cover most "frailty" costs.

confronting people. At one time, "location" meant just that. Simply put, it meant "What part of the country do you want to live in?" Yet today, the expansion of health care options and lifetime learning opportunities, for example, mean numerous new opportunities. "Grandparenting" and access to grandchildren continue as important considerations.

New "Ports of Call" for Retirees?
The Search for Greater Meaning and Value in Retirement

A final point concerns what appears to be a growing trend away from "sunbelt" dominance for retiree living. Two developments are helping to blunt the rush to "sunbelt" locations. First, "Retiring Retirement" means that people are exploring and accessing many more options for "second adulthood" living. Included in this are the number and quality of retirement communities, many of which are situated proximate to the individual's current residence (and family!). Also, a modest but growing number of these are close to or a part of college campuses. University linked communities provide access to stimulating academic environments, mingling with younger students, enjoyment of sports events, convenient health services, and at times, even teaching classes. Some 75 of these university-linked communities are on the drawing board or already exist.

A second consideration blunting the exodus to "sunbelt" communities, aside from the overloading of community services, is the stated intention of many Baby Boomers to keep on working past the old economy retirement marker of 65 years of age. No doubt changing

Social Security eligibility requirements play some part in this picture too. Also, improved health reflected in the person's "Quality Age" is a growing reality and a mitigating factor in the decision to leave the familiar world of work, albeit, part-time or more interesting work may be sought. Thus, if these trends continue, the emphasis will be on staying connected to neighborhoods, friends and/or familiar institutions. "Retirement living' patterns will be less about bridge, canasta, bingo or early-bird specials *as dominant* themes. Volunteerism and continuing education will likely get a huge boost.[3]

"Second Adulthood"; Lifestyle Decision-Making

Logic and intellect alone won't bring you to the "right" or "best" decisions regarding next steps or "What do I do for the rest of my life?" As Carleton Fiorina, President and CEO of Hewlitt-Packard stated, the person has to master the art of listening to his/her head, heart... and gut. Determining what is really possible and gaining a sense of fulfillment and life closure typically lie much *beyond one's immediate choices.* The weight of all that is possible and all that seemingly is not, can create a state of inaction. Inaction, especially in the middle and later stages of second adulthood can drain energy, cause depression and eventually can even be life threatening. Love what you do, although admittedly, the familiar feels comfortable, even attractive. But, do not fail to explore uncharted waters. A case in point is the Elderhostel experience: *It sometimes takes years* to convince a friend that course variety, date/location flexibility, and great teachers are ideally suited to his (their) post work world needs for learning and enjoyment. After "getting their feet wet", many will probably establish some type of record for attending the most Elderhostel sessions in one year!

PUTTING THE LIFE JOURNEY IN PERSPECTIVE

It's only when you stand back and see the whole journey in perspective, the paths chosen, the paths rejected, a pattern emerges, a pattern that over time defines the journey of life.

Carleton Fiorina, President/CEO,
    Hewlitt-Packard Co.
Commencement Speaker, MIT, Cambridge, MA
(May, 2000)

Chapter V – 7

School Was Never Like This:
The New World of Lifelong Learning

THE NEW WORLD OF LIFELONG LEARNING: HAVING FUN AND GROWING, TOO!

In the 1950's it was popularly called continuing education for adults. By the mid 1970's, it had been transformed into the "modern practice of adult education".[1] By the millennium, it had become the *lifelong learning movement.* At mid-century, the appetite for further learning and education was stimulated by the GI Bill which affected millions of World War II veterans. Hundreds of new community colleges, trade schools and universities were established in response to the explosive growth in educational demands. Existing educational units were often overtaxed in trying to cope with the crowds of new "students" on campus.

After the first wave of *adult learners* had largely cleared through the educational system, a distinct change became increasingly clear in the thrust of both the aging adult learners and the "educational system". Conventional (formal) educational facilities could no longer fully satisfy the huge GI generation bulge with traditional course offerings. Wartime physical conditioning of armed forces personnel and rapid advances in health technology benefited both the quality and length of life of individuals. Those who had "saved the world for democracy" were seeking greater meaning and a basis for personal expression in their lives. The educational field's response to these increasingly obvious and growing trends was to conceptualize *adult learner needs, desires* and *preferences* as *andragogy,* as distinct from pedagogy, which was attuned to a much younger student body. *Andragogy's* focus was on the learner first and foremost; then subject matter, teacher and teaching. The "modern practice of

213

adult education" that started to emerge was concerned with a process of self-directed inquiry (see Exhibit V-7 YY). Resources of materials, teachers and even fellow students were available too but not imposed upon the learner. Learners were to have the opportunity to discover for themselves those things which they were ready to

---

EXHIBIT V – 7 YY

BENCHMARKS OF THE NEW LIFELONG LEARNING EXPERIENCE

- Self-directed growth.
  The person takes charge of his or her learning. People master things better than relying on being taught. They are more enthusiastic, have improved retention and exploit it more fully in their lives.

- Adults learn differently than children.
  Their use of experience, sense of time and what is relevant or important is superior for *their* purposes.

- Learning is customized for and by the person.
  No general model fits all or even many. Temperament, stage of life, needs and tastes all affect the particulars.

- Convenience, taste and "what feels comfortable and fun" affect the learning mode and time commitment.

- The worth of any subject area, field, or "learning experience" is a personal matter.

- Timing of the learning experience reflects curiosity or "need to know" as prime motivators. It can take place at virtually any age.

- The *capacity* to learn does not diminish with age, albeit the type of material learned and time to learn it (slower) do change.

- Immersion experiences often accelerate knowledge and skill gains.

- Extraordinary resources surround most all people. These include the home, at work, in the community and exploitation of the computer. The growth of the computer and communications options are extraordinary.

---

explore or discover at a particular phase or stage of their personal development according to Malcolm Knowles (p.15). No wonder that the field of adult learning and education moved rapidly through a transformative period without precedent. An increasingly literate population started to identify continuing learning as an essential part of living and good quality of life (see Exhibit V-7 ZZ). "Lifelong Learners", a term often ascribed to Knowles, seemed wonderfully suited to the new age learner.

Freed at last of traditional (limiting) educational structures and processes, a veritable (and new) alphabet soup of adult materials, learning programs, institutions, processes and arrangements emerged. By the millennium, even adult learning experts were often confused by the multiple directions and complex forms which appeared. (See Exhibit V-7 ZZ at the end of this section for a "lifelong learner's quiz").

The Self-directed Learning Challenge

Many adults are not prepared for self-directed learning. Consequently, they may be unable or unwilling to move through their own discovery or reorienting process. *Learning how to learn and learning new ways to learn represent a threshold that must be crossed* before the wonders and full benefits of lifelong learning can be fully accessed. Key identifying markers of the lifelong learning field include the following:

1. The learner is treated with respect. Memories of classrooms and being treated disrespectfully must be cast aside.

EXHIBIT V – 7 ZZ

THE "WHO WANTS TO" QUIZ FOR THE LIFELONG LEARNER

Who wants to...

Have fun?	Learn new things?
Be challenged?	Get ready to re-career?
Use time well?	Travel to new places?
Feel productive?	Get access to new $$$ making ideas?
Make new friends?	Stay in control of the what,
	when and how?

Any or all of the above are just a few, easy steps away! Take the following *self-quiz* and see if you are ready.

1. There is always something you would like to know more about, learn how to do, or appreciate more or better.

2. New ideas, information, insights and experiences, no matter how modest (e.g., a joke, a recipe or bike riding), are incidents you are willing to pursue.

3. When learning something new or how to do it, "turns you on".

4. Life experiences turn out to be wonderful sources for improved living.

5. Self-learning has been fun and goes much beyond (just) taking courses.

6. A belief that investing time or money in your own growth, personal or occupational, is a sound future investment.

7. Past experience in a continuing education program

Diagnosis: If you answered "yes" to any of the above, the bounty of lifelong learning awaits you.

For added discussion, see a source such as Gross (1977), especially Chapter 1.[2]

2. New "rules" of the game must be learned. The artifacts of classes and learning; e.g., homework, attendance, and taking notes, are typically optional and left up to the adult learner.

3. Learning experiences may be pursued purely for the joy or pleasure they provide to the learner. This contrasts sharply with the work or career focus so often a part of the traditional model. There is no one to whom the individual is accountable other than himself/herself.

4. The venues for lifelong learning are found throughout the community, state, nation and even the world. The sheer number of these and the configurations often assumed can be highly confusing and at times act as a turnoff. In this regard, the personal computer and Web search may prove more confusing than enlightening (more on this shortly). Information overload is quickly reached.

Lifelong Learner Options; A "Sampler"

Some sense of the numerous and wonderful opportunities to be found in the lifelong learning field are described below. All of the descriptions are exclusive of corporate and organization-affiliated (e.g., religious institutions) programs. In addition, they represent only a small selection accessible in a modern, complex city like Chicago and its north and northwest suburbs. Further, with access to computers and television, even remote locations (distance learning) pose no particular barrier in the lifelong learning process.

1. *Oasis.* Established in 1982 in St. Louis by Marylen Mann and Margie Wolcott May, the program now claims a national membership of over 350,000 and is carried out in over 25 cities around the country. A corporate public initiative of the May Company and with initial funding from the Department of Health and Human Services, U. S. Administration on Aging, it has proven to be highly successful. Offerings include challenging programs in the arts, humanities, computers, wellness and volunteer services. The May Department Stores Company (Lord & Taylor in Northbrook, IL) provides dedicated meeting and activity space in most of its stores. The trimester program runs year-round. In Northbrook for example, some 70 different activities are offered each term including the visual arts, music, drama, wellness, history, contemporary issues, consumer affairs, field trips, computers and exercise classes.

2. *North Shore Senior Center* (NSSC). Offers a year-round program of activities including classes, exercise groups, field trips, wellness, computer usage and volunteer services. Each year, thousands of individuals participate in its programs.

3. *Northbrook Community Senior Center.* Very similar to NSSC but focused more particularly on Northbrook residents, its program also includes health awareness days when a variety of health diagnostic services are made available as a community service.

4. *Cancer Wellness Center.* Offers a year-round program (gratis) for people stricken with cancer and their families. Group sessions, exercise groups and a limited number of classes round out its programs.

5. *Bernard Weinger Jewish Community Center* (JCC) of Northbrook. Year-round program of exercise classes and facilities plus a limited number of classes.

6. *Northbrook YMCA.* Courses and a diverse exercise program.

7. *Northwestern University, Evanston, Illinois.* Programs include the Institute for Learning in Retirement (ILR). This type of programming has been called "an educational haven for retirees". Each intellectually stimulating study group consists of 20 or fewer people and a coordinator. Some 20 different subject areas are pursued each term during the regular year; a more limited program is offered during the summer. At present, over 270 college and university affiliated programs are conducted nationally; this is a tremendous increase from the some 20 in 1989.[3] This type of program traces some of its roots back to a program model conceived in 1962 at the New School for Social Research in New York.

Since 1968, the Alumnae of Northwestern University provide a continuing education program serving the greater Evanston community and include many Northwestern University alumni. Each year almost 2000 people from the greater Chicago metropolitan area register for courses at a modest cost.

These types of university affiliated programs have proven so attractive that a whole new wave of retirement communities are being built in conjunction with or proximate to universities including Iowa State, Oberlin College, Stanford, Cornell, Westchester University (PA), Penn State and Eckhard University. Note, the attraction of these programs is suggested by the fact that many lie outside of "sunbelt" states. Residents of university linked communities audit and at times teach classes; they mingle with students and enjoy sports and the arts. Also, intergenerational programs often serve as living laboratories and a basis for research.

8. *Emeritus Program, Oakton Community College.* A long established year-round program providing numerous course offerings in the social sciences, liberal arts, wellness, creative writing and computers. A program motif seems to capture the imagination of the hundreds of older adults attending sessions.

"We shall not cease from exploration, and the end of all our exploring will be to arrive where we started, and know the place for the first time"

9. *Elderhostel.* Although not strictly a "north suburban" program, so many area residents take advantage of their national and international programs that it is worthy of mention. It is so well known that a detailed description is not needed. It is not too unusual for a person (or couple) to have attended 5, 10 or even 20 different programs. A growing number now exceed 100.

10. *Common Ground.* A non-sectarian year-round program of courses dealing with historical, philosophical, religious and current political matters.

11. *Dawn Schuman Institute.* Diverse course offerings, largely from a Jewish perspective.

12. Church and Synagogue Programs. Virtually every major institution offers a year-round program of education for adults.

13. *The Lifelong Learning Society (LLS) of Florida, Atlantic University.* At first blush, Boca Raton, Florida seems very remote from the Illinois-based programs described in this section. Factually, this is true but one of the notable "roosting spots" for area "snowbirds" is the type of area and program provided by Florida Atlantic University (FAU). Proximity to excellent continuing learning facilities is one reason people spend time in or move to the Boca Raton area. Instructors are top-drawer and chosen from many top FAU faculty. Little wonder that the program has grown from some 500 in 1980 to over 12,000 "students" in 2000. In the fall of 1997, LLS moved into its own multi-million dollar plus facility.

THE PERSONAL COMPUTER

The personal computer revolution and its widespread diffusion has upset the crystal ball of futurists predicting the further obsolescence of mature Second Adulthood men and women. A study by the investment firm of Charles Schwab & Company reported that *over 40 percent of people over 50 either own or have access to a computer* (this percent is increasing rapidly). New computer pathways for mature Second Adulthood people, say 55-plus years of age, include an estimated 70% exchanging e-mail, 60% researching specific topics of interest and 50% staying abreast of current events.[4] Additionally, it is estimated that almost one-half of all Net users belong to the Baby Boomer generation.

But the story does not stop with these overall markers of older adults exploiting PC capabilities. Many older adults are reaching for newer, creative uses of the PC including the design of their own greeting cards, desk-top publishing, health management, managing their financial portfolios and accelerating new innovations through membership in computer groups. In fact, the very successful diffusion of PC's has its own built-in dangers. We know a number of adults spending as much as 10 to 15 hours with their PC in a single day! See Chapter 8, Part V for more on the computer.

Chapter V – 8

The Personal Computer and World Wide Web: Your Link to the Future

NEWER PASSAGES AND FUTURE GATEWAYS: TAPPING COMPUTER CAPABILITIES

In the Early decades of the first computer revolution, business and technical applications abounded. Transactional and computational related activities and research were dominant themes of many of these. However, with the second computer revolution featuring PC's and the World Wide Web, *individuals were deeply affected* aside from the great impact on institutional applications. Individuals could now tap the power of information as awesome and novel as any within the institutional or global scene. For example, "Research", often viewed as the domain of scientists, engineers or researchers per se, was now an option for millions of people. If anything, the sheer volume of accessible information was overwhelming and had to be accessed selectively.

For both Baby Boomers and most "Second Adulthooders", the potential impact was enormous. Most all Baby Boomers commanded a range of PC/WWW applications spanning word processing, e-mail, search/scan, and numerous specialized applications such as spreadsheets and desktop publishing. Better than 60 percent of all *mature* "Second Adulthood" people, including those over 65 years of age, commanded most all computer basics including word processing, e-mail and search/scan. In short, the general Second Adulthood population now commanded an information capability that could be readily transformed into knowledge and self-learning. Next jobs, trips, file management, prestigious health centers, health treatment protocols, reliable news, food values, and the latest stock market prices, to name but a few, were now at the fingertips of most "Second Adulthooders". Thus, "stages" or "passages" were no longer passive sociological phenomena anchored in time by social conventions. These had become intervals and "bridges" in a person's life for which even major life cycle markers like marriage, having children, formal education and employment phases, could be greatly shifted and changed in scope or character.

America's New Female Entrepreneurs and CEO's: Computer Wired and Rapidly Expanding

Computer capabilities facilitated an unprecedented era of opportunity for millions of women. For many women, "Second Adulthood" has turned out to be a period of liberation from constraining links to family and homemaker responsibilities. Work related activities could be undertaken at most any place or time. It also meant that tens of thousands of women transitioned out of traditional employment slots and patterns into their own business, virtual offices or ventures. For example, the National Foundation for Women Business Owners estimates that female-owned companies have already surpassed the 9 million mark and are growing quite rapidly. This is the very same time that many men were starting to prepare to gear down and develop new, slower paced lifestyle patterns.

The emergence of an Internet economy with the need for pronounced marketing knowhow and consumer service understandings helped to catalyze these fast expanding female opportunities and developments. These

Internet economy areas were custom made for traditional areas of female strengths.

Computers and the "5 R's"

The PC developments described here fit admirably well with all the components of the "5 R's" described in preceding chapters. "Rest, Recreation, Refuel, Retool and Re-career" all were now more viable options which could be pursued individually, collectively or sequentially. A portion could be opted for at say, age 55, and then the same individual could pursue others in subsequent time periods. Consider the following characteristic computer-application scenarios.

Scenario No. 1; John, a 55 year old Baby Boomer. For "John', the late 40's and early 50's had been a highly intense time. Although his work had paid well and was necessary to put two kids through college, those pressures were now gone. He and his wife wanted a less hectic lifestyle, even to the point of simplifying things by a move into a smaller home and perhaps even a different area. John saw this as an ideal time to "Retool" and 'Re-career" in a different occupational field. Since "Re-career" and "Retool" were seen as important undertakings for the near-term future, the initial computer applications for John might well have involved self-directed aptitude, skill and "career directions" inquiries. Well-developed "WWW" contacts and computer linked programs existed for all of these.

He further pursued the need for "Retooling" through some on-line "distance learning" opportunities. He identified several "cyber" universities and then "signed up" for several on-line learning courses. This arrangement provided the needed flexibility, pacing and quality to satisfy his development of new competencies.

Next, with more specific focus on the types of occupations to be pursued, well-developed job search (computer based) routines and e-mail contacts were used to generate promising leads to newer world-of-work opportunities—most any place in the world! Then, having achieved financial goals much beyond expectations, "Rest" and "Recreation" could take on the mantle of top priority. Literally thousands of possible activities could then be explored ("Researched") using computer capabilities.

The situation confronting Sophie, a 72 year old widow of four years was completely different than John's.

Scenario No. 2; Sophie, a 72 year old widow of four years. She had finally adjusted to her new singles role after the death of her long-term marriage partner. Re-establishing continuity in her life involved continuing visits with grand children, periodic trips (including Elderhostel) with a new friend, and continuing on in her regular Tuesday night card game and three times a week volunteer job at the local hospital. One of her sons who lived out of town insisted that Sophie learn e-mail so that she could stay in touch. The next time he visited with Sophie, they went out shopping, he picked up an inexpensive computer and made arrangements to get her on-line. They then used a neighbor's computer in order to give Sophie a hands-on training session. In just two afternoons she was up and running. Subsequently, her friend offered to teach her a simple word processing program, especially since she served as a "secretary" (minutes) for a church group.

At an annual physical, her doctor indicated that she now had the questionable distinction of being a "Type 2" diabetic. This badly scared her because she had enjoyed quite good health. "Never to worry" said her friend, we'll do some of our own research on the WWW and also go over to the library and see what we can find out there. Both sources proved highly beneficial and Sophie felt far more confident in being able to adjust to and cope with her diabetes.

Scenario No. 3; Ronald and Justine at age 55, had only recently become "empty nesters". Years ago, Justine had taken time out from her job to start a family. Months had stretched into years. However, almost ten years ago she had started thinking about her *freedom* from family responsibilities and return to work. During those same years Ronald had moved through several different jobs but finally settled into one with much less traveling. Both had been involved with PC's for years. Ronald and Justine had both common and individually related computer needs. Their "shared" needs included ticket, hotel and trip arrangements including "bid-ins" on various of these to gain the "lowest price" availability. Many years ago, a friend of Justine had taught her basic computer operations. When she finally outgrew usage of the library computers, *they* set her up with her own computer space in the house. Five years ago, she and her best friend set up a computer oriented home decorating consulting service. She used her computer extensively, subsequently in communications contacts with her partner and following up on leads.

Ronald's PC usage had been more along conventional business related lines such as e-mail, customer quotations, and trouble-shooting problems. One of the "common" computer applications and concerns shared by the couple was a slowly increasing need and desire to research health-related information. Justine had had a bad cancer scare and as a consequence both had become much more familiar with health-related Web sites, computer searches, etc.

* * *

POSTSCRIPT

Retiring Retirement hopefully has opened up some new doors to the wonderful promise and opportunity of *the* Second Adulthood. Good health, happiness and long life is our wish to all of the reading audience.

BIBLIOGRAPHY
and
REFERENCES

BIBLIOGRAPHY AND REFERENCES

Abernathy, Donna J. (1999). "Talking 'Bout Your Generation", in *Training and Development*. November p.20

Achenbaum, W. Andrew (1986). "The Aging of the First New Nation", in Pifer, Alan and Bronte, Lydia, Eds. *Our Aging Society*. NY: Norton: 18-32.

Atchley, Robert C. (1999). *Continuity and Adaptation in Aging: Creating Positive Experiences*. Baltimore: The Johns Hopkins University Press.

Atchley, Robert C. (2000, 9th ed rev). *Social Forces and Aging: An Introduction to Social Gerontology*. Belmont, CA: Wadsworth/Thompson International.

Baltes, Paul B. and Baltes, M. M. (1986). *The Psychology of Control and Aging*. Hillsdale, NJ: Erlbaum.

Benson, Herbert (1975). *The Relaxation Response*. NY: Morrow.

Benson, Herbert with Stark, Marg (1986). *Timeless Healing: The Power and Biology of Belief*. NY: Scribner.

Bloch, Annette and Bloch, Richard (1985). *Fighting Cancer*. Kansas City, MO: R.A. Bloch Cancer Foundation.

Burack, Elmer and Mathys, Nicholas (2001; 4th ed.). *Human Resource Planning*. Northbrook, IL: Brace-Park Press.

Burack, Elmer and Mathys, Nicholas (1988). *Career Management in Organizations.* Northbrook, IL: Brace-Park Press.

Burack, Elmer, Albrecht, Maryann and Seitler, Helene (1980). *Growing: A Woman's guide to Career Satisfaction.* Belmont, CA: Wadswoth and Lifetime Learning. Reprinted, Brace-Park Press.

Burack, Elmer and Torda, Florence (1980). *The Manager's Guide to Change.* Belmont CA: Wadsworth and Lifetime Learning.

Carter, Jimmy (1998). *The Virtues of Aging.* NY: Ballantine.

Chopra, Deepak (1993). *Ageless Body, Timeless Mind: The Quantum Alternative to Growing Old.* NY: Harmony Books.

Chopra, Deepak (1999). *How to Know God: The Soul's Journey into the Mystery of Mysteries.* NY: Harmony Books.

C Q *Researcher.* (1998). "Biology and Behavior: How Much Do Our Genes Drive the Way We Act?". 8, 13: 1-28.

Dossey, Larry (1993). *Healing Words: The Power of Prayer and the Practice of Medicine.* San Francisco, CA: Harper.

Dossey, Larry (1999). *Reinventing Medicine: Beyond Mind-Body to a New Era of Healing.* San Francisco, CA: Harper.

Dychtwald, Ken and Flowers (1989). *Age Wave.* NY: Tarcher/Putnam.

Dychtwald, Ken (1999). *Age Power: How the 21st Century Will Be Ruled by the New Old.* NY: Tarcher/Putnam.

Edelstein, Linda N. 91999). *The Art of Midlife: Courage and Creative Living for Women.* Westport, CT: Bergin & Garvey, Greenwood.

Farrell, Michael and Rosenberg, Stanley D. (1981). *Men at Midlife.* Boston, MA: Auburn House.

Gallup, George Jr. (2000). *The New American Spirituality: Finding God in the 21st Century.* NY: Chariot Victor.

Goleman, Daniel (1995). *Emotional Intelligence.* NY: Harper-Collins.

Goleman, Daniel (1998). *Working with Emotional Intelligence.* NY: Harper-Collins.

Gordon, James S. (1996). *Manifesto for a New Medicine.* Reading, MA: Addison-Wesley.

Graebner, William (1980). *A History of Retirement in the United States.* New Haven, CT: Yale University Press.

Gross, Ronald (1977). *The Lifelong Learner.* NY: Simon and Schuster.

Heller, Richard F. and Heller, Rachael F. (1998). *The Carbohydrate Addict's Lifespan Program.* NY: Plume.

Heller, Richard F., Heller, Rachael F., and Vagnini, Frederick J. (1999). *The Carbohydrate Addict's Healthy Heart Program.* NY: Ballantine.

Knowles, Malcolm S. (1970). *The Modern Practice of Adult Education.* NY: Associated Press.

Korten, David C. (1999). *The Post-Corporate World: Life After Capitalism.* San Francisco: Berrett-Koehler and West, Hartford, CT: Kumariam.

Lachman, Margie E. (1986). "Locus of Control in Aging Research: A Case for Multidimensional and Domain-Specific Assessment". *Psychology and Aging,5*, 1: 34-40.

Lachman, Margie E. and Weaver, Suzanne L. (1998). "Sociodemographic Variations in the Sense of Control by Domain: Findings from the MacArthur Studies of Midlife". *Psychology and Aging,* 13, 4: 553-562.

Lesser, Elizabeth (1999). *The New American Spirituality.* NY: Random House.

McAvay, G. J., Seeman, T. E. and Rodin, J. (1996). "A Longitudinal Study of Change in Domain-Specific Self-Efficacy Among Older Adults". *Journal of Gerontology: Psychological Sciences,* 51B: 243-253.

Mid-life Study (1999). A general reference to the prestigious John D. and Catherine T. MacArthur Foundation Study, covering better than 10 years and reported more recently in various popular press articles and releases.

Murphy, John S. and Hudson, Frederic (1998). *The Joys of Old: A Guide to Successful Elderhood.* Altadena, CA: Goede Press.

Myss, Caroline (1996). *Anatomy of the Spirit: The Seven Stages of Power and Healing.* NY: Crown Publishers.

Neugarten, Bernice L. and Neugarten, Paul A. (1986). "Changing Meanings of Age in the Aging Society", in Pifer and Bronte, Eds., op.cit: 33-51.
Null, Gary (1999). *Gary Null's Ultimate Anti-Aging Program.* NY: Kensington Publishing.

Orloff, Judith (2000). *Guide to Intuitive Healing: Five Steps to Physical, Emotional and Sexual Wellness.* NY: Times Books.

Ornish, Dean (1992). *Dr. Dean Ornish's Program for Reversing Heart Disease Without Drugs or Surgery.* NY: Ballantine.

Pearls, Thomas and Silver, Margery Hutter (1999). *Living to 100: Lessons in Living to Your Maximum Potential at Any Age.* NY: Basic Books.

Pifer, Alan and Bronte, Lydia, Eds. (1986). *Our Aging Society: Paradox and Promise.* NY: W. W. Norton.

Restak, Richard M. (1995). *The Brain and the Mind.* NY: Simon & Schuster.

Restak, Richard M. (1997). *Older & Wiser: How to Maintain Peak Mental Ability for as Long as You Live.* NY: Simon & Schuster.

Roizen, Michael (1999). *Real Age: Are You as Young as You Can Be? An Age Reduction Program That Can Make You Live and Feel up to 26 Years Younger.* NY: Cliff Street, Harper-Collins.

Rowe, John and Kahn, Robert L. (1998). *Successful Aging.* NY: Pantheon.

Schachter-Shalomi, Zalman and Miller, Ronald S. (1995). *From Age-ing to Sage-ing: A Profound New Vision of Growing Older.* NY: Warner Books.

Schwartz, Tony (1995). *What Really Matters: Searching for Wisdom in America.* NY: Bantam Books.

Sheehy, Gail (1995). *New Passages: Mapping Your Life Across Time.* NY: Merritt.

Sheehy, Gail (1998). *Understanding Men's Passages: Discovering the New Map of Men's Lives.* NY: Ballantine.

Siegel, Bernie (1986). *Love, Medicine and Miracles: Lessons Learned About Self-Healing from a Surgeon's Experience with Exceptional Patients.* NY: Harper-Collins.

Simmons, Henry C. and MacBean, E. Graig (2000). *Thriving After 55.* Richmond, VA: Prime Press.

Successful Midlife Development (1998). A research study sponsored by the John D. and Catherine T. MacArthur Foundation, Chicago, IL, covering some ten years and involving better than 3000 people and numerous health personal and behavioral scientists.

Warshofsky, Fred (1999a). *Stealing Time: The New Science of Aging.* NY: TV Books.

Warshofsky, Fred (1999b). "The Methuselah Factor", *Modern Maturity* 42R, 6 November-December: 28-
Weil, Andrew (1995). *Natural Health, Natural Medicine.* NY: Houghton Mifflin.

What to Eat for a Healthy Life (1998). Berkeley, CA: University of California at Berkeley Wellness Letter.

REFERENCE NOTES

I-1: The "Invention" of Retirement and Ageism

1. William Graebner, *History of Retirement in the United States* (New Haven, CT: Yale University Press, 1980).
2. Alan Pifer and Lydia Bronte, Editors, *Our Aging Society: Paradox and Promise* (NY: W.W. Norton, 1986).
3. Gail Sheehy, New Passages: Mapping Your Life Across Time (NY: Merritt, 1995).
4. Zalman Schachter-Shalomi and Ronald Miller, *From Age-ing to Sage-ing: A Profound New Vision of Growing Older* (NY: Warner Books, 1995).
5. Wiliam Graebner, *A History of Retirement in the United States* (New Haven, CT: Yale University Press, 1980): 215.
6. Ibid: 216.
7. Ibid: 225-6.
8. William Graebner, *History of Retirement in the United States* (New Haven, CT: Yale University Press, 1980): 31.
9. Ibid: 71-81.
10. Ibid: 19.
11. Ibid: 95-119.
12. Ibid: 30-35.

I-2: The New "You Bet Your Life" (with apologies to Groucho Marx)

. *CQ Researcher:* Biology and Behavior: How Much Do Our Genes Drive the Way We Act?, 1998: 8, 13: 1-28.

2. Daniel Goleman, *Emotional Intelligence* (NY: Harper Collins, 1995), and *Working with Emotional Intelligence* (NY: Harper Collins, 1998).
3. Deepak Chopra, *Ageless Body, Timeless Mind: A Quantum Alternative to Growing Old* (NY: Harmony Books, 1993). See also Zalman Schachter-Shalomi and Ronald Miller, *From Age-ing to Sage-ing: A Profound New Vision of Growing Older* (NY: Warner Books, 1995), and Bernice L. and Paul A. Neugarten, *Changing Meanings of Age in the Aging Society,* in Pifer and Bronte, Eds., (1986) op. cit.: 33-51.
4. Neugarten and Neugarten, *Changing Meanings of Age in the Aging Society* (1986): 35.

I-3: Profiling the Aging Society

1. Edelstein, Linda N. (1999). *The Art of Midlife: Courage and Creative Living for Women.* Westport, CT: Bergin & Garvey, Greenwood.

II-1: Who's in Charge? Ready or Not, You Are in Charge!

1. Margie Lachman and Suzanne Weaver, "Socio-demographic Variations in the Sense of Control by Domain: Findings from the MacArthur Studies of Midlife", *Psychology and Aging,* (1998), 13, 4: 553-562. See also McAvay, Seeman and Rodin, "A Longitudinal Study of Change in Domain-Specific Self-Efficacy Among Older Adults", *Journal of Gerontology: Psychological Sciences,* (1996), 51B: 243-53, and Baltes and Baltes, *The Psychology of Control and Aging* (Hillsdale, NJ: Erlbaum, 1986).

2. Richard M. Restak, *The Brain and the Mind* (NY: Simon & Schuster, 1995) and *Older and Wiser: How to Maintain Peak Mental Ability for as Long as You Live* (NY: Simon & Schuster, 1997).

3. Margie Lachman and Suzanne Weaver, "Sociodemographic Variations in the Sense of Control by Domain: Findings from the MacArthur Studies of Midlife", *Psychology and Aging*, (1998), 13, 4: 553.

4. Margie Lachman, "Locus of Control in Aging Research: A Case for Multidimensional and Domain-Specific Assessment", *Psychology and Aging*, (1986), 5, 1: 34-40.

5. Deepak Chopra, *Ageless Body, Timeless Mind: The Quantum Alternative to Growing Old*, (NY: Harmony Books, 1993).

6. Mid-life Study (1999). A general reference to the prestigious John D. and Catherine T. MacArthur Foundation Study, covering better than 10 years and reported more recently in various popular press articles and releases.

7. Michael Roizen, *Real Age: Are You as Young as You Can Be? An Age Reduction Program That Can Make You Live and Feel up to 26 Years Younger*, (NY: Cliff Street, Harper-Collins, 1999). See also James S. Gordon, *Manifesto for a New Medicine*, (Reading, MA: Addison-Wesley, 1996), Herbert Benson, *The Relaxation Response*, (NY: Morrow, 1975), Herbert Benson with Marg Stark, *Timeless Healing: The Power and Biology of Belief*, (NY: Scribner, 1986), John Rowe with Robert Kahn, *Successful Aging*, (NY: Pantheon, 1998), Bernie Siegel, *Love, Medicine and Miracles: Lessons Learned About Self-Healing from a Surgeon's Experience with Exceptional Patients*, (NY:

Harper-Collins, 1986), Deepak Chopra, *Ageless Body, Timeless Mind: The Quantum Alternative to Growing Old*, (NY: Harmony Books, 1993), Dean Ornish, *Dr. Dean Ornish's Program for Reversing Heart Disease Without Drugs or Surgery,* (NY: Ballantine, 1992), and Andrew Weil, *Natural Health, Natural Medicine*, (NY: Houghton Mifflin, 1995).

8. Mid-life Study, op.cit., (1999).

9. James Gordon, *Manifesto for a New Medicine,* (Reading, MA: Addison-Wesley, 1996).

10. Ibid: 241.

11. Ibid: 241.

12. Zalman Schachter-Shalomi and Ronald Miller, *From Age-ing to Sage-ing: A Profound New Vision of Growing Older,* (NY: Warner Books, 1995).

13. *Nutrition Action Health Letter,* 1999: 2.

14. *Journal of the American Medical Association,* 1997: 277 & 472.

II-2: How Old Are You Really? Quality Age

1. Michael Roizen, *Real Age,* (NY: Cliff Street, Harper-Collins, 1999): 10.

2. Alan Pifer and Lydia Bronte, Eds., *Our Aging Society: Paradox and Promise,* (NY: W.W. Norton, 1986). See also Ken Dychtwald, *Age Wave,* (NY: Tarcher/Putnam, 1989), Gail Sheehy, *New Passages: Mapping Your Life Across Time,* (NY: Merritt, 1995), Richard M. Restak, *Older and Wiser,* (NY: Simon & Schuster, 1997), Mid-life Study (1999), and Michael Roizen, *Real Age,* (NY: Cliff Street, Harper-Collins, 1999).

3. Andrew Achenbaum, (1980): 16.

4. Neugarten & Neugarten, "Changing Meanings of Age

in the Aging Society", in Pifer and Bronte, Eds., (1986): 33-39.

5. Ibid: 35.

6. Ibid: 35.

7. Successful Mid-life Development (1998), a research study sponsored by the John D. and Catherine T. MacArthur Foundation, Chicago, IL, covering some ten years and involving better than 3000 people and numerous health and behavioral scientists.

8. Gail Sheehy (1996). See also Schachter-Shalomi (1995) and Chopra (1993).

9. Ken Dychtwald, *Age Wave*, (NY: Tarcher/Putnam, 1989). See also Roizen (1998): Introduction.

II-3: Characteristics of "Second Adulthood People": A Newer View of Age and Aging

1. Especially Schacther-Shalomi (1995), Chopra (1995), Goleman (1995 and 1998), and Roizen (1999).

2. Daniel Goleman, *Emotional Intelligence*, (NY: Harper-Collins, 1995), and *Working With Emotional Intelligence*, (NY: Harper-Collins, 1998).

3. Michael Roizen, *Real Age*, (NY: Cliff Street, Harper-Collins, 1999).

III-1: Mapping Health Success Strategies: Background

1. Thomas Perls and Margery Hutter Silver, *Living to 100: Lessons in Living to Your Maximum Potential at Any Age,* (NY: Basic Books, 1999).

2. Fred Warshofsky, "The Methuselah Factor", *Modern Maturity* 42R, 6, November-December 1999: 84.

III-2: Mapping Health Success Strategies: Methods

1. Dr. Irwin Weil, *Breathing* (1999). See also Herbert Benson, *The Relaxation Response* (NY: Morrow, 1975).
2. Michael Roizen, *Real Age,* (NY: Cliff Street, Harper-Collins, 1999).

III-4: Mapping Health Success Strategies: Numerical Approaches (Part 1)

1. Michael Roizen, *Real Age,* (NY: Cliff Street, Harper-Collins, 1999).
2. Ibid: book jacket.
3. Ibid: esp. 20-42.

IV-1: Trip Planning

1. Elmer Burack and Florence Torda, *The Manager's Guide to Change,* (Belmont CA and Lifetime Learning, 1980).
2. Richard F. and Rachael F. Heller and Frederick J. Vagnini, *The Carbohydrate Addict's Healthy Heart Program,* (NY: Ballantine, 1999): 72.
3. Heller, Heller and Vagnini (1999). See also Heller and Heller, *The Carbohydrate Addict's Lifespan Program,* (NY: Plume, 1998) and Deepak Chopra, *Ageless Body, Timeless Mind,* (NY: Harmony Books, 1993).
4. Heller & Heller (1998), and Heller, Heller and Vagnini (1999).
5. Heller, Heller & Vagnini (1999): Introduction, 1-70.

6. Elizabeth Lesser, *The New American Spirituality,* (NY: Random House, 1999): 92.

7. Chopra (1993). See also Heller, Heller and Vagnini (1999), Richard Restak, *Older and Wiser: How to Maintain Peak Mental Ability for as Long as You Live,* (NY: Simon & Schuster, 1997), James S. Gordon, *Manifesto for a New Medicine,* (Reading, MA: Addison-Wesley, 1996), Herbert Benson (1996), Andrew Weil, *Natural Health, Natural Medicine* (NY: Houghton Mifflin, 1995), and Larry Dossey, *Healing Words: The Power of Prayer and the Practice of Medicine,* (San Francisco, CA: Harper, 1993).

8. Chopra (1993): 36-37.

9. Ibid: 32.

IV-2: A Framework for Personal Change

1. Elmer Burack and Florence Torda, *The Manager's Guide to Change,* (Belmont CH and Lifetime Learning, 1980. See also Burack and Nicholas Mathys, *Human Resource Planning,* (Northbrook, IL: Brace Park Press, 2001, 4th Edition).

2. Richard and Rachael Heller and Frederick J. Vagnini, *The Carbohydrate Addict's Healthy Heart Program,* (NY: Ballantine, 1999). See also Heller and Heller, *The Carbohydrate Addict's Lifespan Program,* (NY: Plume, 1998).

V-1: Introduction to the "5 R's", Lifestyle and Financial Security Planning

1. Mid-life Study (1999), MacArthur Foundation.

V-2: The Financials, Health Care and Women's Issues

1. Medicare Beneficiary Survey (1996).
2. *Working Age,* 1998. 14, 4, November-December.
3. *New York Times,* September 12, 1999: A1 and A14.
4. *Working Age,* 1998. A special issue on women and saving for retirement.
5. *Focus on Health,* 1999.
6. *Business Week,* July 1999.
7. *Chicago Tribune,* September 1999: 1.
8. Based on calculations in Ellis (1997) and Simmons and MacBean (2000).
9. *Fortune,* August 17, 1998: Foldout.

V-3: Spirituality

1. George Gallup, Jr., *The New American Spirituality: Finding God in the 21st Century,* (NY: Chariot Victor, 2000).
2. Elizabeth Lesser, *The New American Spirituality*, (NY: Random House, 1999): 4-5.
3. Gallup (2000). See also Judith Orloff, *Guide to Intuitive Healing: Five Steps to Physical, Emotional and Sexual Wellness,* (NY: Times Books, 2000).
4. Orloff (2000).
5. Lesser (1999).
6. Ibid: 5-7.

7. Ibid: 5-7.

8. Deepak Chopra (2000).

9. Deepak Chopra, *How to Know God: The Soul's Journey into the Mystery of Mysteries,* (NY: Harmony Books, 1999): 53.

10. Herbert Benson, *The Relaxation Response,* (NY: Morrow, 1975) and Benson with Marg Stark (1986). *Timeless Healing.* NY: Scribner.(1996).

11. Zalman Schachter-Shalomi, *From Age-ing to Sage-ing: A Profound New Vision of Growing Older,* (NY: Warner Books, 1995).

12. Ibid.

13. Ibid: 2-4.

14. Ibid: 5.

15. John S. Murphy and Frederic Hudson, *The Joys of Old: A Guide to Successful Elderhood,* (Altadena, CA: Goede Press, 1998).

16. Schachter-Shalomi (1995), Chopra (1999), Gallup (2000) and Lesser (1999).

17. Murphy and Hudson (1998), and Orloff (2000).

V-4: A New "Track"

1. Gail Sheehy, *New Passages: Mapping Your Life Across Time,* (NY: Merritt, 1995): 5-10.

2. Robert C. Atchley, *Continuity and Adaptation in Aging: Creating Positive Experiences,* (Baltimore, MD: The Johns Hopkins University Press, 1999).

3. Ibid: 155.

4. David C. Korten, *The Post-Corporate World: Life After Capitalism,* (San Francisco: Berrett-Koehler and West Hartford, CT: Kumariam, 1999): 3.

V-5: Planning for a "Second Adulthood"

1. Gail Sheehy, *New Passages: Mapping Your Life Across Time,* (NY: Merritt, 1995).
2. Michael Roizen, *Real Age,* (NY: Cliff Street, Harper-Collins, 1999). See also Sheehy (1995), and Sheehy, *Understanding Men's Passages: Discovering the New Map of Men's Lives,* (NY: Ballantine, 1998).
3. Zalman Schachter-Shalomi and Ronald S. Miller, *From Age-ing to Sage-ing: A Profound New Vision of Growing Older,* (NY: Warner Books, 1995): 52-77.
4. Herbert Benson (1986).

V-6: Sorting Things Out and Making Decisions

1. Henry C. Simmons and Craig E. MacBean, *Thriving After 55,* (Richmond, VA: Prime Press, 2000).
2. Ibid: 140-3. See also the Mayo Clinic Health Letters (1998).
3. Business Week, July 12, 1999.

V-7: School Was Never Like This: The New World of Lifelong Learning

1. Malcolm S. Knowles, *The Modern Practice of Adult Education,* (NY: Associated Press, 1970).
2. Ronald Gross, *The Lifelong Learner,* (NY: Simon & Schuster, 1977), esp. Chapter 1.
3. *New York Times,* December 26, 1999: 12.
4. Donna J. Abernathy, "Talking 'Bout Your Generation", in *Training and Development,* November 1999: 20.